Discover the Northern Adirondacks

Four-Season Excursions from
Lake Placid, Saranac Lake and Points North

Barbara McMartin
Patricia Collier
James C. Dawson
Phil Gallos
Peter O'Shea

Prepared with the assistance of E.H. Ketchledge

Backcountry Publications
Woodstock, Vermont

An Invitation to the Reader
Over time trails can be rerouted and signs and landmarks altered. If you find that changes have occurred on the routes described in this book, please let us know so that corrections may be made in future editions. The author and publisher also welcome other comments and suggestions. Address all correspondence to:

Editor
Discover the Adirondacks Series
Backcountry Publications
P.O. Box 175
Woodstock, VT 05091

Library of Congress Cataloging-in-Publication Data

Discover the Northern Adirondacks

   (Discover the Adirondacks series)
   Bibliography: p.
   Includes index.
   1. Adirondack Park (N.Y.)—Description and travel—
Guide-books. 2. Outdoor recreation—New York (State)
—Adirondack Park—Guide-books. I. McMartin, Barbara.
II. Ketchledge, Edwin H. III. Series.
F127.A2D57 1988   917.47'530443   88-26300
ISBN 0-942440-46-3 (pbk.)

Published by Backcountry Publications
A division of The Countryman Press, Inc.
Woodstock, Vermont 05091

Printed in the United States of America by McNaughton & Gunn
Typesetting by The Sant Bani Press
Series design by Leslie Fry
Layout by Barbara McMartin
Maps by Richard Widhu

Photograph credits
Phil Gallos, cover, 70, 111, 116, 123, 143, 153, 159, 163, 166
Patricia Collier, 6, 21, 23, 28, 39, 40, 43, 54, 66, 74, 146, 180, 219
James C. Dawson, 183, 185, 191, 198, 200, 203, 213
E. H. Ketchledge, 59, 63
Chuck Brumley, 114, 128, 130, 132
Edythe Robbins, 2, 195, 196
Ruth Rosevear, 94
Barbara McMartin, 52, 82

Photographs
Cover: *High Peaks view from Seymour*
Page 2: *Bridge over Ray Brook on Scarface Trail*
Page 6: *View from Ebeneezer*

Discover the
Northern Adirondacks

Four-Season Excursions from
Lake Placid, Saranac Lake and Points North

Acknowledgements

This guide differs from several in the Discover series in that most of the friends who have worked with me on it have done so as coauthors. Their work on this guide was wonderful, their dedication to the project was perfect, and I am indebted to all of them.

Fran Rosevear, historian for the series, researched Coney Mountain and its background. Morris F. Glenn provided historical material on the mine areas.

Brian McDonnell helped describe the new cross-country ski network near Saranac. With Jack Drury, Brian researched the wonderful trail from Lake Oseetah to Averyville.

Charles Knox Brumley planned to write for this guide but his life has taken a new direction that prevented his participation. Nevertheless, some of his writing and pictures have found their way into this book, and they are much appreciated.

Gary Hodson and Peter Fish of DEC helped us with current trail information. W. Garry Ives, Margaret Baldwin, and Terry Healey of DEC assisted Jim Dawson in his investigations. Peter O'Shea relied on the help of Jim Papero.

Jim Dawson was accompanied by his wife, Caroline, on some of his hikes. Pat Collier was accompanied by Gwenne Rippon, Virginia Durso, Roger Menges, and Jean Spatny.

Edythe Robbins came through again. With Chuck Bennett, she managed a last-minute trip to help us finish the guide.

W. Alec Reid printed all the photographs except those taken by Phil Gallos. Alec even got out of the darkroom long enough to make a couple hikes.

Ed Ketchledge walked quite a few trails and sent tape-recorded notes. His insights were invaluable.

Additions and corrections in this revised printing were made by Phil Capone, retired Regional Forester from Ray Brook, who has extensive knowledge of the trails in this guide. His efforts are greatly appreciated.

Contents

Introduction

WHAT IS SPECIAL about hiking or skiing in the northern Adirondacks? Are the northern slopes of the mountain dome really different from the rest of the Adirondack Park? The answer is unequivocally yes. Every guide I work on has had a distinct flavor. One of the more rewarding aspects of guidebook writing is trying to distill each region in a brief description that will not only lead the reader to an understanding of the area but will spark a desire to know more of it.

The northern Adirondack region was shaped by farming, mining, industry, railroads, fires, and guides who entertained visitors from eastern cities. The northern side of the mountain range was settled almost as early as the eastern regions, before parts of the southern Adirondacks even.

Before the last quarter of the nineteenth century, however, the settlements were very small. The first northern railroad, the Lake Champlain and Ogdensburg, built in 1845, made commerce possible in the lowlands to the north of the Adirondacks. Before the end of the century, railroads were laid out from Plattsburgh west past the town of Dannemora and Lyon Mountain. The Chateaugay Railroad reached Saranac Lake in 1887 and Lake Placid in 1893. The Northern Adirondack or Hurd's Railroad reached south from Malone to Tupper Lake by 1889. Webb's Mohawk and Malone, or the Adirondack and St. Lawrence, was completed in 1892.

Ashes from the coal burning engines of these early trains were dumped at trackside, sparks spewed from their stacks. In the drought years that followed the completion of the railroads, trains caused most of the disastrous fires. In 1903, for instance, fires along the New York Central (successor to Webb's railroad) and the Saranac and Lake Placid lines devastated half a million acres, causing an enormous loss of timber. Six thousand men worked to put out these fires.

Iron mines or forges at North Elba, Ausable Forks, Dannemora, and Lyon Mountain changed the face of the countryside because of the vast forests of hardwoods harvested to produce charcoal. These places all play a role in various hikes.

Routes described in this guide are along abandoned railroad tracks, through land cut over for charcoal, and along the carries used by early guides to travel between ponds. Most of the region's summits are and were wooded. Lumbering and fires cleared some peaks. Verplanck Colvin ordered the clearing of a number of peaks that he needed for his survey work.

A few of the routes are trails cut expressly for the hiker, for by the last quarter of the nineteenth century, mountain climbing was in vogue. Many level routes are along marked trails, but unfortunately the majority of the mountains, especially many of the little, peripheral ones with superb views, are trailless, and for them this guide describes bushwhacks that range from the very easy to the extremely difficult.

The western portion of this guide is the fabled lake district, and routes here follow the railroad and the numerous carries that link the numerous ponds and lakes. This guide describes some of the carries as hikes and many more as links in cross-country ski loops that make use of the frozen surfaces of the ponds and lakes. For more details about canoeing the region, consult Paul Jamieson's *Adirondack Canoe Waters, North Flow*, which also includes a rich historical background of the region.

This guide includes a capsule history of the territory surrounding each hike or group of hikes. But, most intriguing of all, are the centers of the region's two Wilderness Areas, small mountain ranges, with almost no human history and no answer to the riddle, why were they passed by?

How to Use the Discover Guides

The regional guides in the *Discover the Adirondacks* series will tell you enough about each area so that you can enjoy it in many different ways at any time of year. Each guide will acquaint you with that region's access roads and trailheads, its trails and unmarked paths, some bushwhack routes and canoe trips, and its best picnic spots, campsites, and ski-touring routes. At the same time, the guides will introduce you to valleys, mountains, cliffs, scenic views, lakes, streams, and a myriad of other natural features.

Some of the destinations are within walking distance of the major highways that ring the areas, while others are miles deep into the wilderness. Each description will enable you to determine the best excursion for you and to enjoy the natural features you will pass, whether you are on a summer day hike or a winter ski-touring trek. The sections are grouped in chapters according to their access points. Each chapter contains a brief introduction to that area's history and the old settlements and industries that have all but disappeared into the wilderness. Throughout the guide you will find accounts of the geological forces that shaped features of the land, mention of unusual wildflowers, and descriptions of forest stands.

It is our hope that you will find this guide not only an invitation to know and enjoy the woods but a companion for all your adventures there.

MAPS AND NOMENCLATURE

The *Adirondack Atlas*, a map published by City Street Directory of Poughkeepsie, New York, is the best reference for town roads, and it has the added advantage of identifying state land. In spite of the fact that it has not been updated to show recent acquisitions, this is a valuable aid where public and private lands are intricately mixed. The new *Adirondack North Country Regional Map* shows all state land, including purchases made through 1986. Copies may be obtained free of charge as long as the supply lasts by contacting the Adirondack North Country Association, P.O. Box 148, Saranac Avenue, Lake Placid, NY 12946, phone 518-523-9820.

The widely separated parcels of state land in the region covered by this guide mean that a large number of U. S. Geological Survey (USGS) quadrangles are needed to cover all the routes. The base maps are all 7.5-minute sheets or the new metric maps. Maps in this guide are adequate for the routes described, but you may want to purchase some of the metrics. The majority of maps in this guide are reproduced at fifty percent reductions, so 1 mile = 1⅜ inches. A few are reproduced full scale for greater detail for some of the bushwhacks. *Note that where metric and 7.5-minute maps have been juxtaposed, the different maps have different contour intervals.*

The USGS base maps are Keene Valley, Ampersand Lake, Tupper Lake, Lake Placid, Saranac Lake, Upper Saranac Lake, Wilmington, Bloomingdale, and St. Regis Mountain metric quadrangles, and Lake Ozonia, Meno, Ellenburg Depot, Ellenburg Mountain, Dannemora, Lyon Mountain, Owls Head, Lake Titus, Meacham Lake, Debar Mountain, Alder Brook, and Redford 7.5-minute quadrangles.

Maps are available locally in many sporting goods stores. You can order maps from USGS Map Distribution Branch, Box 25286, Denver Federal Center, Denver, CO 80225. They are currently more easily obtained from a private source, Timely Discount Topos. You can call them at 1-800-821-7609; with your credit card number they will ship maps within a week.

The guide uses the spelling given in the USGS but local variations are noted.

DISTANCE AND TIME

Distance along the routes is measured from the USGS survey maps and is accurate to within ten percent. It is given in miles, feet, or yards except where local signs use metric measure. Distance is a variable factor in comparing routes along paths or bushwhacks. Few hikers gauge distance accurately even on well-defined trails.

Time is given as an additional gauge for the length of routes. This provides a better understanding of the difficulty of the terrain, the change of elevation, and the problems of finding a suitable course. Average time for walking trails is 2 miles an hour, 3 miles if the way is level and well defined; for paths, 1½ to 2 miles an hour; and for bushwhacks, 1 mile an hour.

Vertical rise usually refers to the change in elevation along a route up a single hill or mountain; *elevation change* generally refers to the cumulative change in elevation where a route crosses several hills or mountains.

A line stating distance, time, and vertical rise or elevation change is given with the title of each section describing trails and most paths, but not for less distinct paths and bushwhacks for which such information is too variable to summarize. Distance and times are for *one way only*, unless otherwise stated. The text tells you how to put together several routes into a longer trek that will occupy a day or more.

TYPES OF ROUTES

Each section of this guide generally describes a route or a place. Included in the descriptions are such basic information as the suitability for different levels of woods experience, walking (or skiing, paddling, and climbing) times, distances, directions to the access, and, of course, directions along the route itself. The following definitions clarify the terms used in this book.

A route is considered a *trail* if it is so designated by the New York State Department of Environmental Conservation (DEC). This means the trail is routinely cleared by DEC or volunteer groups and adequately marked with official DEC disks. *Blue disks* generally indicate major north-south routes, *red disks* indicate east-west routes, and *yellow disks* indicate side trails. This scheme is not, however, applied consistently throughout the Adirondacks.

Some trails have been marked for *cross-country skiing*, and new *pale yellow disks with a skier* are used. *Large orange disks* indicate *snowmobile trails*, which are limited to some portions of Wild Forest Areas. Snowmobiles are permitted on them in winter when there is sufficient snow cover. The guide indicates trails not heavily used where skiing and snowmobiling may be compatible, but a skier must always be cautious on a snowmobile trail. Hikers can enjoy both ski and snowmobile trails.

A *path* is an informal and unmarked route with a clearly defined foot tread. These traditional routes, worn by fishermen and hunters to favorite spots, are great for hiking. A path, however, is not necessarily kept open, and fallen trees and new growth sometimes obliterate its course. The paths that cross wet meadows or open fields often become concealed by lush growth. You should always carry a map and compass when you are following an unmarked path and you should keep track of your location.

There is a safe prescription for walking paths. In a group of three or more hikers, stringing out along a narrow path will permit the leader to scout until the path disappears, at which point at least one member of the party should still be standing on an obvious part of the path. If that hiker remains standing while those in front range out to find the path, the whole group can continue safely after a matter of moments.

Hikers in the north country often use the term *bushwhack* to describe an uncharted and unmarked trip. Sometimes bushwhacking literally means pushing brush aside, but it usually connotes a variety of cross-country walks.

Bushwhacks are an important part of this regional guide series because of the shortage of marked trails throughout much of the Adirondack Park and the abundance of little-known and highly desirable destinations for which no visible routes exist. Although experienced bushwhackers may reach these destinations with not much more help than the knowledge of their location, I think most hikers will appreciate these simple descriptions that point out the easiest and most interesting routes and the possible pitfalls. In general, descriptions for bushwhacks are less detailed than those for paths or trails; it is assumed that those who bushwhack have a greater knowledge of the woods than those who walk marked routes.

Bushwhack is defined as any trip on which you make your way through the woods without a trail, path, or the visible foot tread of other hikers and without markings, signs, or blazes. It also means you will make your way by following a route chosen on a contour map, aided by a compass, using streambeds, valleys, abandoned roads, and obvious ridges as guides. Most bushwhacks require navigating by both contour map and compass, and an understanding of the terrain.

Bushwhack distances are not given in precise tenths of a mile. They are estimates representing the shortest distance one could travel between points. This reinforces the fact that each hiker's cross-country route will be different, yielding different mileages. Some of this guide's shorter bushwhacks are calibrated in yards traveled, hopefully making them more suitable for the novice bushwhacker.

A bushwhack is said to be *easy* if the route is along a stream, a lakeshore, a reasonably obvious abandoned roadway, or some similarly well-defined feature. A short route to the summit of a hill or a small mountain can often be easy. A bushwhack is termed *moderate* if a simple route can be defined on a contour map and followed with the aid of a compass. Previous experience is necessary. A bushwhack is rated *difficult* if it entails a complex route, necessitating advanced knowledge of navigation by compass and reading contour maps and land features.

Compass directions are given in degrees from magnetic north and in degrees from true north. The text will usually specify which reference is used, but if no reference is given the degrees refer to magnetic north.

The guide occasionally refers to old *blazed* lines or trails. The word "blaze" comes from the French *blesser* and means to cut or wound. Early loggers and settlers made deep slashes in good-sized trees with an axe to mark property lines and trails. Hunters and fishermen have also often made slashes with knives and, though they are not as deep as axe cuts, they can still be seen. *It is now, and has been for many years, illegal to deface trees in the Forest Preserve in this manner.* Following an old blazed path for miles in dense woods is often a challenging but good way to reach a trailless destination.

You may see *yellow paint daubs on a line of trees.* These lines usually indicate the boundary between private and public lands. Individuals have also used different colors of paint to mark informal routes from time to time. Although it is not legal to mark trails on state land, this guide does refer to such informally marked paths.

All *vehicular traffic,* except snowmobiles on their designated trails, is *prohibited* in the Forest Preserve. Vehicles are allowed on town roads and some roads that pass through state land to reach private inholdings. These roads are described in the guide, and soon the DEC will start marking those old roads that are open to vehicles. Most old roads referred to here are town or logging roads that were abandoned when the land around them became part of the Forest Preserve. Now they are routes for hikers, not for vehicles.

There has been an increase in the use of three- and four-wheeled off-road vehicles, even on trails where such use is prohibited. New laws have gone a long way toward stopping this in the Forest Preserve, ensuring that some of the old roads remain attractive hiking routes.

The *beginning of each section describing a trail* gives a summary of the distance, time, and elevation change for the trail. For unmarked routes, such information is given only within the text of each section—partly to allow for the great variations in the way hikers approach an unmarked route, and partly to emphasize the difficulty of those routes.

Protecting the Land

Most of the land described in these guides is in the *Forest Preserve,* land set aside a century ago. No trees may be cut on this state land. All of it is open to the public. The *Adirondack Park Agency* has responsibility for the Wilderness, Primitive, and Wild Forest guidelines that govern use of the Forest Preserve. Care and custody of these state lands is left to the Department of Environmental Conservation, which is in the process of producing Unit Management Plans for the roughly 130 separate Forest Preserve areas.

Camping is permitted throughout the public lands except at elevations above 4000 feet and within 150 feet of water or 100 feet of trails. In certain fragile areas, camping is restricted to specific locations, and the state is using a new No Camping disk to mark fragile spots. *Permits* for camping on state lands are needed only for stays that exceed three days or for groups of more than ten campers. Permits can be obtained from the local rangers, who are listed in the area phone books under New York State Department of Environmental Conservation.

Only dead and downed wood can be used for *campfires.* Build fires only when absolutely necessary; carry a small stove for cooking. Build fires at designated fire rings or on rocks or gravel. Fire is dangerous and can travel rapidly through the duff or organic soil, burning roots and spreading through the forest. Douse fires with water, and be sure they are completely out and cold before you leave.

Private lands are generally not open to the public, though some individuals have granted public access across their land to state land. It is always wise to ask before crossing private lands. Be very respectful of private landowners so that public access will continue to be granted. Never enter private lands that have been posted unless you have the owner's permission. Unless the text expressly identifies an area as state-owned Forest Preserve or private land whose owner permits unrestricted public passage, the inclusion of a walk description in this guide does not imply public right-of-way.

Burn combustible trash and carry out everything else.

Most *wildflowers and ferns* mentioned in the text are protected by law. Do not pick them or try to transplant them.

Safety in the Woods

It is best *not to walk alone*. Make sure someone knows where you are heading and when you are expected back.

Carry water or other liquids with you. Not only are the mountains dry, but the recent spread of *Giardia* makes many streams suspect. I have an aluminum fuel bottle especially for carrying water; it is virtually indestructible and has a deep screw that prevents leaking.

Carry a small *day pack* with insect repellent, flashlight, first aid kit, emergency food rations, waterproof matches, jackknife, whistle, rain gear, and a wool sweater, even for summer hiking. Wear layers of wool and waterproof clothing in winter and carry an extra sweater and socks. If you plan to camp, consult a good outfitter or a camping organization for the essentials. Better yet, make your first few trips with an experienced leader or with a guide.

Always carry a *map and compass*. You may also want to carry an altimeter to judge your progress on bushwhack climbs.

Wear *glasses* when bushwhacking. The risk to your eyes of a small protruding branch makes this a necessity.

Carry *binoculars* for birding as well as for viewing distant peaks.

Use great care near the *edges of cliffs* and when *crossing streams* by hopping rocks in the streambed. Never bushwhack unless you have gained a measure of woods experience. If you are a novice in the out-of-doors, join a hiking group or hire the services of one of the many outfitters in the north country. As you get to know the land, you can progress from the standard trails to the more difficult and more satisfyingly remote routes. Then you will really begin to discover the Adirondacks.

The Sentinel Range

IN SPITE OF the familiarity of its three-summit profile as the backdrop for postcards and television views of the Lake Placid Ski Jump, the Sentinel Range is one of the least known Wilderness Areas in the park. With the exception of Pitchoff on the southern border, all its peaks are trailless. One series of short trails circles three small ponds on the northwestern border of the area. Two notch trails, parts of longer loop ski trails constructed for the 1932 Olympics, remain. One valley trail, a portion of the original State Road from Northwest Bay to Hopkinton, has been revived as a part of the ski-touring network from Keene to Saranac.

Even Verplanck Colvin did not visit these secreted peaks until late in his career as state surveyor. It was not until 1895 that a signal-tower was erected on Kilburn Mountain (Colvin's Sentinel), the high middle peak in the range.

Sentinel Peak, east of the main range is a prominent landmark from NY 9N and the East Branch Valley, but it and the three principal peaks of the main range are bushwhacks offering limited views at best. All but one of the shorter peaks in the Sentinels are reached by long and difficult bushwhacks, hence only that one is described in this guide. Instead, shorter, easier, more rewarding peripheral bushwhacks in other areas are included. The fact that the Sentinel Mountains are without views has left its interior one of the least disturbed and untouched of the Adirondack's mountainous wilderness areas.

1 Pitchoff Mountain

Hiking, snowshoeing
4.5 miles, 4 to 6 hours, 2000-foot elevation change, map I

To fully appreciate this mountain, you should hike its trail from end to end over all five of its rocky summits. The beginning is your choice. The mountain's two trailheads are 2.8 miles apart, and the trail is marked with red DEC markers.

Just southwest of Cascade lakes on NY 73 there is a fairly good-sized parking turnout that serves hikers for Cascade and Porter on the one side of the road and Pitchoff on the other side. If you start from here, cross the road to the northwest side, climb up the steep bank, and start along the trail north through a mixed forest of maple, birch, hemlock, and spruce.

In a few minutes, the trail veers to the east. For the entire way across the five summits, your trail direction ranges between north and east. In a few minutes more, an open ledge off to the right of the trail allows views of Cascade Mountain and Upper Cascade Lake. A bit farther on, another open ledge on the right gives you a more extensive view—it now includes Algonquin and Colden mountains.

After thirty minutes, unless you have stopped to enjoy the views, at about 1 mile, you come to a trail junction. The official trail goes left. The trail right, a precipitous route to the first summit, is closed off and considered unsafe. The route left leads you around to the north behind the first summit and in another fifteen minutes you reach a path that leads you right, safely, to it along a two-minute detour. There is a large, open expanse of rock to explore with two balancing rocks marking the far end of the summit. From here you can see Marcy, Big Slide, and Hurricane mountains.

Retracing your steps to the trail junction, you continue northeast. You work your way through a stand of small balsam threatening to engulf the trail. This leads to the second summit where Haystack, Basin, Gothics, Armstrong, and Upper Wolf Jaw come into view. From a ledge between the second and third summits you can see Whiteface and Giant. In this stretch, you will also notice some old Conservation Department markers.

Continue generally on the ridge line until summit number four. Beyond it, the markers are yellow painted slashes on rocks and trees, red DEC markers, and yellow painted, plain markers. You have a steep drop plus a chimney to maneuver as you descend from this summit. There are boulders aplenty all the way along the ridge line, but the fifth summit has the most, and they are the most fun to get around and over. Continue east along the open rock, then too soon, you are off this summit and heading for the lower trailhead. Barely discernible here just below the summit is an old path going just north of east to the Old Military Road.

The trail swings south now and is steep and eroded. The deciduous forest is of birch, beech, and maple. Your descent moderates as you approach the road. The lower trailhead is 5 miles west of Keene, and there is little space for parking here.

Although the entire trip can be done in under four hours, allow a couple of hours more so that you can savor each of the summit areas.

View toward Colden and MacIntyre from Pitchoff

2 Old Military Road
Hiking, cross-country skiing, fishing
3.5 miles one way, 2 hours, 650-foot elevation change, map I

This picturesque trail was once, from about 1810 until the late 1850s, the only direct highway from Keene and the east to North Elba and the west. The present road along the Cascade Lakes was authorized in 1858. The summit of the original route through the narrow pass is at about 2350-feet elevation, as compared with 2200 feet for the Cascade Road.

Donaldson's *History of the Adirondacks* clearly shows that the route was never a military road, but the name persists. The trail along the route of the road west from Keene Valley has been incorporated into the new trail system of the Adirondack Ski Touring Council. Eventually, their trail will reach from Keene to Tupper Lake, and this is the first leg to be completed in that network.

The picturesque high mountain notch is a deep, wet, mossy valley with numerous beaver ponds in varying stages, some of which often flood the trail. But it is only because of these open ponds and meadows that you can enjoy the spectacular views of the wild northern cliffs and crags on Pitchoff that overhang the route.

Whether you start from the east or west end of the trail is a personal choice, though there is nearly 500 feet more downhill if you head east. The decision is made easier if you make a round trip. It is short enough so that retracing your steps through the notch does not make a difficult trip.

The eastern trailhead is at the end of Alstead Hill Road, 3 miles from its beginning which is 0.8 mile west of Keene on NY 73. (Note that the USGS gives this as Alstead Mill, but local signs say Hill, which is used here.) The western trailhead is 0.8 mile west of the Mount Van Hoevenburg Recreation Center. Turn north on a dirt road, following it for 1 mile to a small parking area. This can be muddy in spring, especially a spot 0.3 mile short of the trailhead.

The Alstead Hill Road Trailhead is in a pretty meadow with a view of the High Peaks. Starting from this end, you follow Nichols Brook on the old roadbed. Not very far along, you cross a wide plank bridge just above the convergence of two brooks. There is now a gradual climb. In 1.0 mile, you come out of the woods onto an old beaver dam across a large pond. The pond is filled with stumps and dead trees, a number of boulders, and a beaver lodge. You can find natural brook trout here.

Pond along Old Military Road beneath Pitchoff Cliffs

To the south looms Pitchoff Mountain. You can see the mountain along most of the trail—either you have open views from the beaver ponds, or you catch glimpses through the trees.

As you reenter the woods, there is yet evidence of the roadbed. About 0.5 mile west of the pond, your way narrows to a footpath. The next three beaver ponds, not quite as depicted on the most recent USGS map and certain to change again, come in close succession. These too are filled with stumps and tall dead trees and have beaver lodges. Before reaching the last pond, notice the beautiful deep valley south of the trail. You are climbing the side of a hill and just a few feet left of the trail the hillside drops sharply away into this valley. At 2.5 miles you begin a gentle descent from the height-of-land toward the last pond.

At the last pond, at 2.75 miles, take time for a break. You look straight up at the tree-covered rock wall of Pitchoff. It is impressive. Just beyond, close to the left side of the trail, just below the cliffs, is gargantuan Shelter Rock. This huge boulder has fallen from the rock wall of Pitchoff. Hikers often walk just this far, coming from the west, to enjoy a picnic on the rock. From it you have a wonderful view of the pass and of the mountain; you can even spot the place on the flanks of Pitchoff from which the boulder fell.

Continuing west, you might find water over stretches of the trail. If so, take the high road north of the trail on a fairly well-defined herd path. This last section is a pleasant open woods with several kinds of birch, beech, and an occasional hemlock. A gentle descent brings you to the western trailhead.

3 South Notch

Hiking, cross-country skiing
3.3 miles one way, 1³/4 hours, 1150-foot ascent, map 1

The beginning of this trail is a mess. Lumbering has torn up the whole area. Even the trail sign has been cut down. Left of the trail on a rise is a very nice lean-to. It is private and not for public use.

At 0.4 mile, when you enter the Sentinel Wilderness Area, all evidence of devastation ends. The trail, defined by red DEC markers, follows a pretty tributary of Roaring Brook for not quite half the distance to another lean-to (this one public, maintained by DEC) at the end of the trail, but short of the notch.

To reach the trailhead, turn north on Riverside Drive from NY 73 near the ski jump south of Lake Placid. In 2 miles you reach the trailhead, but there is only space for parking along the side of the road.

Just before you enter the wilderness area, there is an elaborate bridge over Roaring Brook. This walkway leads to Camelot's back door. Camelot is a boy's home operated by the Catholic Church.

Sporadic red markers delineate the route. Just short of 1.2 miles, you cross a tributary of the brook on a slippery log bridge to walk along its right bank. In a few minutes, you cross again on another log bridge. In spring, this is a wet trail—wear waterproof boots. The next brook crossover, at 1.4 miles, is nice—on rocks.

A lush understory of fern, witchhopple, and flowers lies beneath a mixed forest of hemlock, spruce, maple, birch, and beech. It makes for a pretty walk. It is a shame that the end of the trail, at 2.7 miles with just under 1000 feet of climbing, is nowhere—simply in the middle of an open woods at a rickety lean-to.

A likelier end to this trail would be 0.5 mile farther on at the top of the notch or even on the Old Military Road trail. Otherwise, the South Notch Trail probably will fade away and become history. It is, however, an easy bushwhack through open woods to the notch, and for the adventurous, this is the place to start a 0.5-mile bushwhack north up Slide Mountain, which has some of the steepest slopes in the range.

4 North Notch

Hiking, cross-country skiing
2.7 miles one way, 1 1/2 hours, 1150-foot ascent, map I

This little used trail takes you into the heart of the Sentinel Wilderness Area and the best place from which to plan a bushwhack to Kilburn's double summit. The route to the notch is easy, and the round-trip distance is 5.4 miles on a DEC red-marked trail.

There is a good-sized turnout for cars on the east side of Riverside Drive. To reach it from the south, turn right off NY 73 by the ski jump south of Lake Placid. Go 3.0 miles to the North Notch Trail. From the north, you turn south off NY 86 onto Riverside Drive and continue for 1.0 mile. This is a pretty drive following the West Branch of the Ausable River. Take time to enjoy the views of the Sentinels, Whiteface, and the High Peaks. This is a popular place for bicycling and fishing.

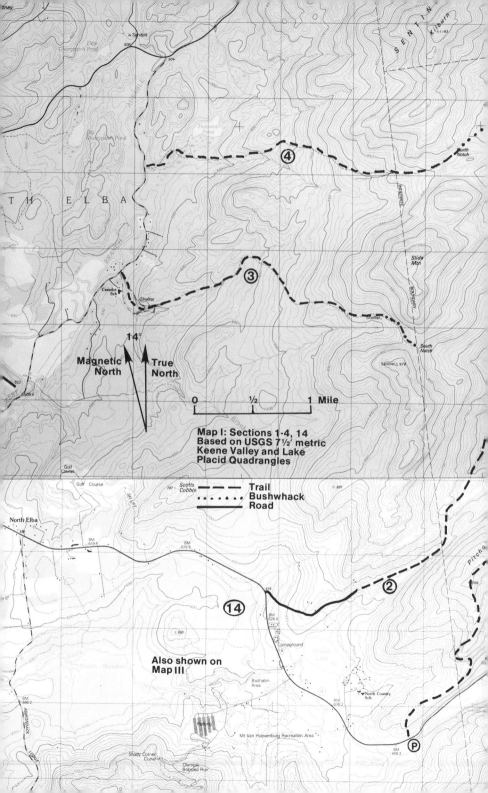

Map I: Sections 1-4, 14
Based on USGS 7½' metric
Keene Valley and Lake
Placid Quadrangles

14°

Magnetic North   True North

0   ½   1 Mile

- - - - Trail
········ Bushwhack
─────── Road

Also shown on
Map III

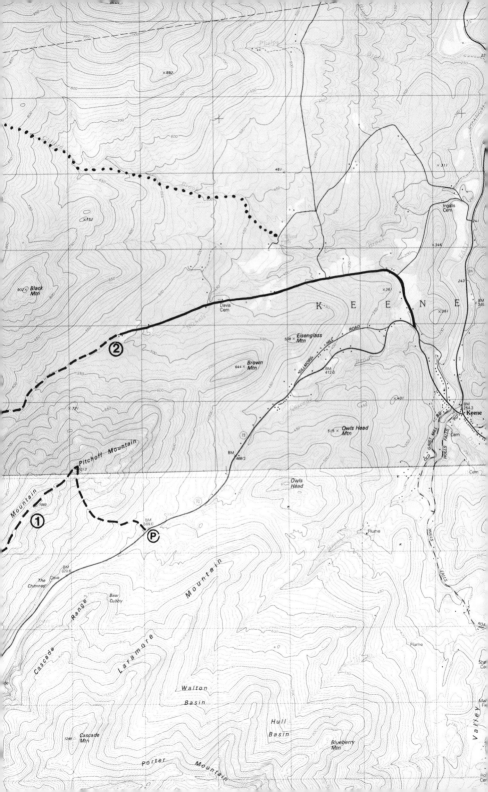

Copperas Pond

A brook that combines several small drainages from Slide Mountain, North Notch, and Holcomb Pond flows into the Ausable here near the trailhead. The trail leaves the road on the north side of the brook. In a minute it veers left to avoid a swampy area, crossing a dip with a broken log bridge over it. The trail meanders around and about and up and down, through the hemlocks with an occasional birch popping up. In ten minutes, at 0.4 mile, you come to a wetland that is filling in with trees. In the winter, you can see Kilburn Mountain from here.

After walking on the level beside the wetland and crossing a small brook, at 0.8 mile you begin an easy ascent that continues pretty much to the end of the trail. There is an abundance of ferns, flowers, wood sorrel, and meadow rue. You keep leaving and returning to the brook, crossing it on assorted log bridges. Most of this brook from the Notch is not even shown on the updated USGS. In some areas, although you cannot see the brook, you can hear its music.

As you climb farther into the wilderness, you can sense, before seeing, the mountains rising on either side of the trail. Slide Mountain is to the south, and Kilburn Mountain is to the north.

The maintained trail ends at a level area just before you would cross the brook. For another 0.5 mile, square blue markers guide the adventuresome hiker to the top of the notch. And from there, you can bushwhack northeast to Clifford Brook, following it to the road, on the other side of which is Clifford Falls. Just before reaching the road, you cross private property. Stay near the brook and be respectful of private property.

If you decide to make the through trip from Riverside Drive to Clifford Falls, you need to leave a car near the falls. Head west from Keene on NY 73 and turn on Alstead Hill Road, then turn right on Bartlett Road. Go 0.6 mile before making a left onto Clifford Falls Road. You come to the bend in the road where you can spot a car or two in 0.5 mile. It is a 0.25-mile walk to the falls from this spot. The bushwhack adds 3.5 miles to the 3.2-mile walk to the Notch from the west.

For the avid bushwhacker who wishes to use this approach to Kilburn, note first that there are cliffs facing southwest from Kilburn's southern summit. However, this has been described as a horrible bushwhack because of the thick cover. It is best left to the experts, who need little help planning the trip.

5 Copperas, Owen, Winch, and Marsh Ponds

Hiking, swimming, picnicking, fishing
Trails: Blue – 1.8 miles, Yellow – 0.5 mile, Red – 0.4 mile, 2 hours, 200-foot elevation change, map III

The wonderfully scenic NY 86 between Lake Placid and Wilmington offers several lovely hiking trails. At one point, the West Branch of the Ausable River, which is very popular for fishing, is close to the north side of the road and to the south is a rock wall. A gap in this rock wall affords you access to a complex of trails connecting three lovely ponds. Each pond is different from the others and well worth visiting.

Two trailheads serve the network. The northern trailhead with a good-sized parking area is 2.8 miles southwest of Whiteface Mountain Ski Center and 6.4 miles northeast of the intersection of NY 73 and 86 in Lake Placid. A second trailhead is 1 mile southwest of the northern one. The trail from the southern one is a fairly easy route leading first to Owen Pond.

A blue-marked trail connects the two trailheads and leads past Copperas and Owen ponds. The trails leading to Winch Pond suggest a short loop from the northern trailhead.

From the north, the trail takes right off and UP. In 0.2 mile, over 200 feet above the road, you reach a trail junction. The way right leads to Copperas Pond and left to Winch Pond. If you turn right, in another two minutes on the main DEC blue trail you crest the hill and start sharply down. You are over the rock wall.

You come out of the wood on the northeast corner of Copperas Pond, 0.2 mile beyond the junction. At this point there is a path leading west to a lean-to that is in excellent condition. Along the way, there are great boulders at the water's edge—a nice place for resting, swimming, and picnicking.

This is a marvelous little pond, encircled with trees right to shoreline—cedar, birch, pine, hemlock, beech, and spruce. There is sheep laurel among the rocks all along this north shore.

Returning to the main trail, you continue along the edge of the pond for 0.1 mile. Here you can take the yellow trail 0.5 mile straight ahead to Winch Pond. In 0.4 mile, a red trail goes left for 0.4 mile, mostly on the level, to rejoin the main trail 0.2 mile from the highway, for a short loop after you have visited Winch Pond.

The 0.5 mile to Winch Pond on the yellow trail is a lovely, peaceful walk through the woods. Winch is a wild little pond with dead trees in the water all along the shore. Quite a few water lilies dot the pond. An old Conservation Department sign says this is "special brook trout water" where "the use of fish as bait either alive or dead is prohibited."

Retracing your steps to Copperas Pond, you turn left. A split log walkway carries you 75 feet over a corner of the pond. Soon, 0.1 mile, you arrive at a clearing with a gorgeous view of Whiteface Mountain.

Until recently there was a lean-to here. DEC has removed it because of its proximity to the road. The fate of the lean-to on the north shore is in doubt.

From this point, continuing south, you reach Owen Pond in 0.6 mile. It is the largest of the three. As on Copperas, the cedars predominate on the shore. Walk 0.2 mile along the north shore, then follow the outlet brook through a hemlock grove for 0.5 mile back to the highway. The outlet brook crosses under the road and empties into the West Branch of the Ausable River.

If you spotted a car here, you can ride back to the Copperas Pond Trailhead. If not, it is a very enjoyable 1-mile walk along the river.

A wonderful extension of a visit to Owen Pond is the 1.25-mile bushwhack northeast of the pond to the valley between the Sentinel Range and Wilmington Notch. Two small streams flow into the eastern side of Owen Pond. You want the northern of the two, which is almost at the northeast corner of the pond, less than 200 yards south from the trail where it starts to swing north toward Copperas Pond.

Follow the stream, taking its right branch (the left is the outlet of Winch Pond). Head up the valley toward Marsh Pond; there is no way to get lost on this bushwhack for the walls on either side of the valley keep you from straying more than 100 yards. At the eastern end of marshes, near the outlet brook, you can find a place from which to view the surrounding mountains. Marsh Pond is a shallow body of water beyond the marshes, and it has a dense shoreline. This remote spot, a total of 2 miles from the highway, is right at the foot of Stewart Mountain, walled in by steep slopes.

Marsh Pond and the beaver meadows southwest of it provide the most intimate and imposing view of the major peaks of the Sentinel Range. The view of Stewart Mountain to the east is especially striking because this compact peak practically leaps up from the narrow valley that holds the pond. Kilburn's demeanor is different. It is a little more distant and rises like a tremendous wall to the southeast and south. Between these two mountains, you can catch a glimpse of the summit ridge of Sentinel Peak. The prevailing feeling at Marsh Pond, so surprisingly close, as the crow flies, to a major highway corridor, is one of deep remoteness. The steep, dark, spruce-clad slopes of the mountains, their summits bristling with cripple-bush, convey a sense of palpable aloofness that both tantalizes and threatens the would-be explorer of those high regions. You will not be the first to sit by the shore of this quiet pond, looking up at the range that is the heart of this wilderness, and say to yourself, "Not today ... but someday."

6 Cobble Mountain
Bushwhack, map II

This wonderful little mountain lies off the beaten path. It is an easy, 0.6-mile hike to the summit and, like so many small peaks, it offers outstanding views. Even the road approaches to the beginning of the route offer nice views.

From the crossroads in Keene, you drive 0.8 mile northwest on NY 73 to Alstead Hill Road. Take it for 1.1 miles, then turn right onto Bartlett Road. You reach the trailhead in another 2.5 miles, and there is room off

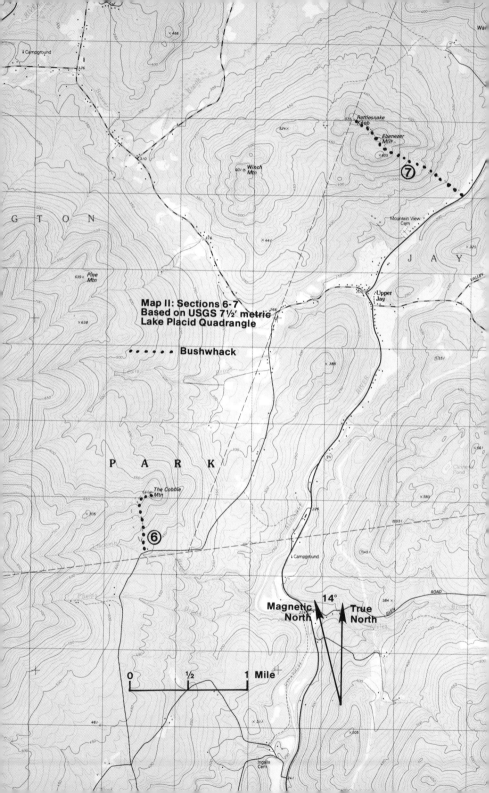

**Map II: Sections 6-7
Based on USGS 7½' metric
Lake Placid Quadrangle**

• • • • • • → Bushwhack

⑦

⑥

14°

Magnetic
North

True
North

0   ½   1 Mile

the west side of the road for one or two cars. Alternatively, from the north and Upper Jay, take Springfield Road north for 0.8 mile and turn left on Bartlett Road for 2.6 miles to the beginning.

There is a discernible path north for a short way. Then you bushwhack, continuing north, through open deciduous forest—mostly beech. You climb fairly steeply for about 0.15 mile to a ridge. Follow this ridge north on a faint herd path. Here on the ridge there are a few hemlock, white pine, and spruce among the beech trees, with spring flowers beneath. As you climb, turn around and view Noonmark and Dix through the trees.

You follow the ridge up for 0.25 mile before dipping slightly—at this point, you are heading east. Then it is straight up over the rocks. Take a breather on a lookout rock part way up. From Sentinel in the west extending to many of the High Peaks around to the south and the Ausable Valley in the southeast, the view is spectacular. Directly in front of you are the colorful beech and red pines.

From Sentinel, moving south, lie Algonquin, Pitchoff, Cascade, Porter, the Brothers, the beginning of the Great Range, Nippletop and the Dials, Dix, Noonmark, and Round mountains. Scrambling the rest of the way to the summit, you add Giant and Hurricane to your view.

There is a bit of summit area to explore, for blueberries in season as well as vistas. As you move east, you can see the Jay Mountain Wilderness Area. Rather than going over the rocks, you can bear north and pick up a herd path to the summit. There are no views on this route until you reach the final destination, but it is a less difficult way to do this last 0.1 mile.

The one-way distance for this bushwhack is just over 0.6 mile in a 600-foot climb. Allow over two hours for the round trip so you have time to enjoy the summit.

7 Ebenezer and Rattlesnake
Bushwhack, map II

As you approach Upper Jay, traveling north on NY 9N from Keene, you see a small mountain looming directly behind the town. This is Ebenezer. One rocky area near the summit is noticeable. People who have lived here all their lives call this area the "ball" or "face."

From Upper Jay, you continue on NY 9N for 1.2 miles to a parking area on the southeast side of the road. Directly across from it, you can walk through a field to the woods. This field is private as is the entire summit, and you are walking here with the owner's consent. Take good care of this access so permission to use it will continue.

You need a map and compass because there is very little evidence of herd paths. Bear west-northwest (approximately 295° true, or 310° magnetic) more or less all the way over Ebenezer Mountain to Rattlesnake Knob.

Plant life on Ebenezer is similar to that found in the lower elevations (the Adirondack foothills). Because of the rich, sweet soil, you will find basswood, oak, maple, white pine, ironwood, dogwood, white ash, and jack pine. This is about the southern limit of the range for jack pine. Its distinctive cones seem to remain on the trees forever. You will find dead branches festooned with these cones, which require such high temperatures to force them open that they only regenerate after a fire.

The cover includes pyrola, poison ivy, maidenhair fern, white baneberry, wild grape, wild ginger, pipsissewa, rose twisted stalk, Christmas fern, mayapple, snakeroot, bedstraw, herb robert, bluebell, coreopsis, corydalis, witch hazel, flowering raspberry, and maple viburnum. This would make good farmland and appears to have been used as such in the nineteenth century.

You cross three tote roads in fairly quick succession within a few minutes of starting your ascent. It is not long before you see the cliffs. You parallel the cliffs, staying south and out away from them, until you get quite near the summit. At that point, you walk close to the cliff, then head north up and over the rocks onto the face. Your views are of the Jays and Sentinels and surrounding peaks.

You walk west along the ridge (called Perkins Ridge by natives), dipping once before arriving at another open area. From it you have a gorgeous view of Whiteface. From here, it is 0.3 mile to Rattlesnake. You drop steeply off Ebenezer to the col, but your way up Rattlesnake Knob is gradual. Again, you get a wonderful view of Whiteface. Now all you have to do is find your way back the way you came.

The summit of Ebenezer (1975 feet) is almost 1300 feet above the road and a bit more than a mile from it. This is a steep little mountain! So allow plenty of time because the trip takes longer than you would imagine, at least four hours for the 3-mile round-trip bushwhack. It can be a real adventure and test your abilities as a woodsperson.

Near Lake Placid

LAKE PLACID, THE village, sits on the shores of Mirror Lake, which is not connected with Lake Placid, the lake, to the north, though the outlets of both are joined in the Chubb River, a tributary of the West Branch of the Ausable. Southeast of the lakes is a broad valley surrounded by the most scenic mountains in the Adirondack Park.

The first settlement, in 1809, grew up around Archibald MacIntyre's Elba Iron Works on the Chubb River. That enterprise failed, and in 1840, only six families lived in the Town of North Elba. They were farmers whose farms occupied the high valley, part of which was known as the Plains of Abraham. Among those who farmed the plains was John Brown, the abolitionist, whose farm and grave has been preserved as an historical site.

Here as elsewhere in the north country, farmers began to entertain visitors, guide them to the surrounding lakes and streams, and expand their homes to "hotels." Robert Scott and Joseph V. Nash were among the first whose homes evolved in this way. The first real hotel, the first Lake Placid Inn, was built by Benjamin T. Brewster in 1871, a watershed year in the growth of the village. The inn encompassed 450 acres, including a peninsula at the south end of Lake Placid and part of Cobble Hill, section 8. In 1876, Nash built a second hotel, the Excelsior, which like most was consumed by fire, this one in 1887.

Among the many wealthy or influential men attracted to Lake Placid was Melville Dewey, founder of the American Librarian Association and advocate of spelling reform. In 1895 he directed the beginning of the Lake Placid Club, an exclusive club on 5 acres on the east shore of Mirror Lake. This soon grew to cover 200 adjoining acres, golf courses, four clubhouses, 72 cottages, and 7800 nearby acres of forest and farms. By 1919, the Inn had over 1200 guests with nearly 750 employees. Most important, in 1904, it began to stay open through the winter.

From this beginning has grown the sports capital of the Adirondacks, indeed, of the eastern part of the United States. Hotels, ski slopes, skating rinks, and golf courses, the developed trappings of recreation abound. However, just a few minutes from the village, there remain many beautiful hiking trails, some described in this chapter, others in the chapters on Whiteface and the McKenzie Wilderness Area.

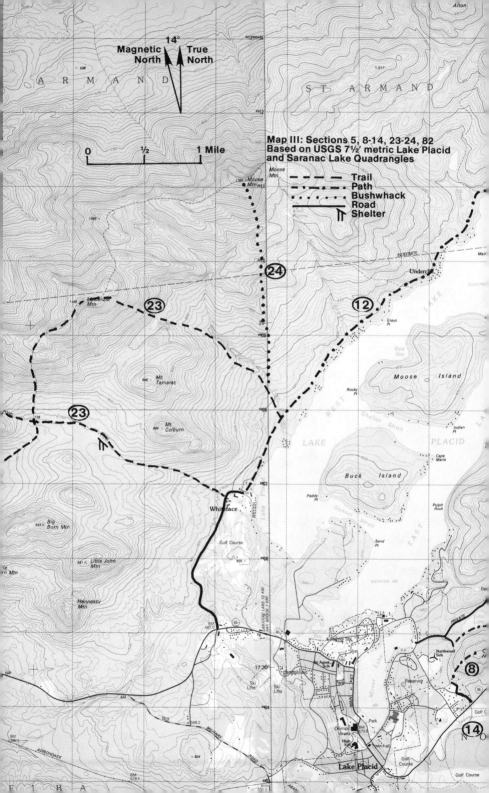

Map III: Sections 5, 8-14, 23-24, 82
Based on USGS 7½′ metric Lake Placid
and Saranac Lake Quadrangles

14°
Magnetic North
True North

0   ½   1 Mile

Trail — — —
Path — ·— ·—
Bushwhack · · · · ·
Road ······
Shelter

Also shown
on Map XIX

Also shown
on Map I

8 Cobble Hill

Path, hiking
0.4 mile, ½ hour, 460-foot vertical rise, map III

This small mountain overlooks the village of Lake Placid and rises less than 500 feet above the lake. From Riverside Drive, head south on NY 86 to Cobble Hill Road. From the intersection of NY 73 and 86, drive 1.1 miles east on NY 86 to the road and turn left, north, on it. In 0.3 mile turn right onto a narrow roadway. In 0.1 mile there is a grassy area on the left large enough for one or two cars to be parked. This is private land, and the owner gives permission to cross. Respect the land so that permission continues. Most of the top of the mountain, however, is state land.

There is a double white pine on the right and a single one on the left of the path's beginning. You pass close to a house on the left of the path. The path is marked with red paint and heads just east of north through a mixed forest.

In a few minutes, you pass a closed off path on the left. Be sure to note this so that you avoid it on the descent. In another few minutes, you pass another path on the left. By now, your way has veered around to the east, then south, and quickly east again.

In fifteen minutes, you get a view from a rock ledge of the MacIntyre Range, and Colden, Marcy, Scarface, Haystack, and McKenzie mountains. Continuing to climb, you reach a junction two minutes above the ledge. Left leads down, your path is up to the right. Thirty minutes in all gets you to the summit from which you can see Basin, Saddleback, and Gothics in addition to those visible from below.

The broad view is little changed from 1917, when T. Morris Longstreth wrote about it in *The Adirondacks*.

"It was the most astounding ten minutes' worth of climb that I have ever done. And many times since have I been up the Cobble, once with thunder stalking down the valley, often with the spruces showing black against deep snow, and always there has been some measure of surprise at such a view from such a tiny hill. . . . Below us lay the road that wound from the Notch which partly showed to the northeast. The Notch was steeped in shadow; but the sheer range of the Sentinel Mountains, still lighted by the level sun, streamed southward from it, making a barrier all along the east of the valley, an abrupt limit to its beautiful floor. On the south the greater mountains, Elephant, Saddleback, Basin, Haystack, Tahawus, Algonquin, and colder Iroquois stood remote, but clearly high. On the west nearer mountains continued the valley's wall to the break wherein the Saranacs lie. With the proper sun their glimmer can be caught. Again to the northwest McKenzie, Moose, and St. Armand rose protectingly. In the north Whiteface, always noble dominated. At his foot lay Lake Placid, balsam-girt, islanded."

Little Cherrypatch Pond, Whiteface in the background

In several places to the right of your path going up, you can find evidence of an old chair lift for a downhill ski run. Remember on the way down to keep bearing left. For a small amount of work and time, your rewards are great. This mountain top and the views are very special.

9 Big Cherrypatch Pond

Path, hiking, fishing
0.5 mile, 15 minutes, level, map III

South of NY 86 is a pine needle-covered path leading to this wonderful, little known pond, whose approach and shorelines are now state land. There is a good-sized turnout for cars 2.4 miles east of the intersection of NY 73 and 86 in Lake Placid and 0.9 mile west of Riverside Drive.

The path begins 100 yards east of the parking turnout. Mostly level, it pretty much follows the outlet brook. You are traveling through a coniferous forest interspersed with a very few hardwoods.

Halfway to the pond, a side path leads you to the outlet brook, which, at this point, is flooded and held back by a beaver dam. The main path ends in 0.5 mile on a knoll overlooking the pond. A rock fireplace and two rusty grills hanging from a dead hemlock indicate fishing was popular here.

Connery Pond

Twenty feet off the knoll is a beaver lodge. A narrow peninsula covered with cat-o-nine tails juts out from the eastern shore and is a relatively short distance in front of your knoll. The pond is surrounded by evergreens. It is a lovely, peaceful spot.

10 Connery Pond

Hiking, fishing, cross-country skiing
0.6 mile, 20 minutes, relatively level, map III

There is fishing access to Connery Pond along a road that serves several private dwellings. You will start along this route if you walk on to Whiteface Landing or Whiteface Mountain. Since you are crossing private land, it is important to stay on the trail.

The walk to Connery Pond begins from a parking area on the west side of NY 86, 3 miles north of Lake Placid Village or 0.2 mile south of the junction of Riverside Drive and NY 86. A DEC guide board marks the parking area. Head north along the road/trail. Several driveways to private land turn from it. At 0.5 mile, the trail veers west to round Connery Pond. At 0.9 mile, just short of cables that prohibit vehicular traffic, a path forks east to the pond. The southern and western shores of the pond are privately owned, but the north and east shores are state land.

11 Whiteface Landing

Hiking, cross-country skiing
3.1 miles, 1¹/₂ hours, relatively level, map III

A trail leads from NY 86 to Whiteface Landing on the northeast shore of
Lake Placid. Start as for Connery Pond, section 10, and at 1 mile continue
by walking past the triple steel bar at the boundary of state land. The trail
now follows an abandoned logging road that was used to clean up downed
timber after the 1950 hurricane. As you leave Connery Pond you begin a
walk through quiet, open hardwoods, survivors of that blowdown.

The trail gains and loses 200 feet in gradual elevation changes as it heads
north. At 3 miles there is a junction. Straight ahead is the Shore Owner's
Association Trail that circles Lake Placid. It used to lead to Eagle Eyrie,
which is on state land. Right is the red trail to Whiteface, section 83. Turn
left for 0.1 mile to Whiteface Landing from which there is a view down the
shore of the west arm of the lake past Hawk, Moose, and Buck islands.
Note that power boats that ply the lake can bring hikers to this point.

12 Shore Owners Association Trails

Hiking, cross-country skiing, map III

The Shore Owners Association (SOA) of Lake Placid maintained many
trails around the lake and in the nearby mountains. See the chapter on the
McKenzie Wilderness for more details of the association and its trails.
Currently only one trail along the west shore of Lake Placid remains, and
it is only visible in places.

From Lake Placid, head west on NY 86 to the top of the rise leaving the
village and turn right, north, on Whiteface Inn Road. In 1.5 miles there is
a sign for the Whiteface Resort Golf and Country Club and across from
the sign on the left, Chipmunk Lane leads 0.1 mile to a turnaround and
parking. From the turnaround dip 150 feet to the lake and a sign for the
SOA trail, which contains a map of the lake and a list of the private
property owners around the lake. It also states that the SOA provides a
beautiful trail for members and for all others; the public may use it at the
owner's pleasure and at the visitor's risk.

The Lake Trail follows the west shore north, generally never out of sight
of the lake, so it is impossible to get lost. Occasionally, signs pointing to

the Lake Trail direct you away from private property. The trail reaches the turnoff to McKenzie Mountain, section 24, in 0.6 mile, and shortly beyond crosses Two Brooks. There is no bridge here, so crossing is limited to low water times. In another mile, the trail crosses Minnow Brook, then at about 3 miles, reaches Falls Brook. Side trails used to lead from the Lake Trail to the cascades on Falls Brook. Today, this is a bushwhack destination.

The trail, intermittent today, continues to circle the north shore of Echo Bay, and just short of 4 miles crosses a brook on the east side of which a second side trail headed north leads to Eagle Eyrie. This trail is also faint to nonexistent, mostly because the view from Eagle Eyrie is increasingly grown in and restricted. Hikers wishing to reach this point of takeoff for Eagle Eyrie might better paddle to Whiteface Landing or walk there along the trail from Connery Pond, section 11. The Lake Trail is well inland as it heads east from Echo Bay to just north of Whiteface Landing. Eagle Eyrie is about 0.5 mile from the brook crossing and about 800 feet above the lake. The east shore Lake Trail seems to have been supplanted by the route from Connery Pond.

13 Echo Pond

Path, cross-country skiing, hiking
1.5 miles one way, 1 hour, moderate grades, map III

This is a bit out of the ordinary. Rather than the pond's being your destination, you start your trip just west of the pond and go through the woods back to NY 86. The round trip makes a pleasant way to get a couple hour's exercise. Besides it is an excuse to explore the road past Mount Whitney with its lovely views, areas the natives enjoy. (The maps call it Echo Lake, but everyone says pond, so this guide will also.)

From NY 73 and 86 in Lake Placid, go 0.25 mile west on Main Street. Turn right on Lake Placid Club Drive and make another right turn in 1.1 miles onto Mount Whitney Road. There is no sign here; it is the road beyond Northwood Road.

Mount Whitney Road dead ends at some private homes on Lake Placid. The Lake Placid Club's ski lodge is 0.5 mile before the end of the public road. It is well worth the 2.2-mile drive to the lodge. On the way, you have a gorgeous view of Whiteface and Wilmington Notch.

Actually, your trailhead is only 0.35 mile from the beginning of Mount Whitney Road. The only parking is along side the road. The path is on the

Mount Whitney Road view toward Whiteface

right, south, and you head east on it. In two minutes you arrive at a junction. The path right would bring you to a three-way intersection: left to the Echo Pond, right to Cobble Hill Road, the middle to Cobble Hill, with most of the routes on private land. You should take the left turn at the first intersection. This path stays on the level and shortly you are traveling along the shore of the pond. The route is colorfully marked with lavender wooden squares.

At the far end of the pond, you reach another junction. Straight ahead would take you to Mount Whitney Road. Your path goes right and shortly is skirting the back side of Cobble Hill. In a minute or two you pass another path that leads right and up that hill.

You are now following red can-top markers in a mostly deciduous forest. At the halfway point, you will notice a red wooden diagonal-shaped marker to the left of the path, just beyond a downed tree across the path. Your route now diverges from the marked path, which also comes out on Mount Whitney Road. Both paths go east; the marked path left, slightly north of east and your path right, slightly south of east. The route is relatively level to NY 86.

If you want to start from NY 86, there is a good-sized pull off on the south side of the road 1.6 miles west of Riverside Drive and 1.6 miles east of NY 73 and 86 in Lake Placid. From the parking area you walk east for 0.3 mile to the marked path.

14   Jackrabbit Ski Trails near Lake Placid
Cross-country skiing, maps I and III

The Adirondack Ski Touring Council has designed a trail from Keene Valley west to Lake Placid and Saranac Lake. The Jackrabbit System will eventually reach all the way to Tupper Lake with side loops and will encompass over 100 miles of trails. Its blue guide boards are appearing at road crossings throughout the region. The trail is named for Herman "Jackrabbit" Johannsen a native of Norway who worked to promote ski touring in the Lake Placid region from 1916 to 1928, laying out some of the trails now incorporated in the long eponymous route.

Some of the trails are on Forest Preserve land and are not groomed. The Old Military Road Trail, section 2, from Keene Valley to the Cascade Ski Touring Center on NY 73 is one of those sections. No fees are charged for the portions through state land, which serve also as hiking trails in summer. However, there are fees for skiing at the Cascade Center as well as the privately run trails on the Craig Wood Golf Course (30 kilometers on the fairways) and Whiteface Resort. At present tickets from one area are honored at most of the others. All these areas have groomed trails. Brochures and maps are available at all the centers and throughout the resort area. This guide will only describe those portions of the trail system in the Forest Preserve.

Mount Van Hoevenburg has a dense network of ski trails run by the Olympic Regional Development Authority. This complex is south of NY 73 and ranges up the slopes of that mountain. A fee is charged for skiing the trails, which are not open to hiking during the summer, even though this is state land.

The Adirondack Ski Touring Council's brochure describes the 6-mile Lake Placid to Cascade Ski Touring Center Trail. Its high points include magnificent views from the Craig Wood Golf Course toward Whiteface and the McKenzie Range.

The Lake Placid (Whiteface Resort) to Saranac Lake Trail (McKenzie Pond Road) is described in the Saranac Lake chapter, section 17.

Near Saranac Lake

FARMERS, GUIDES, AND hotel keepers were the first residents of Saranac Lake. Jacob Smith Moody settled there in 1819 and fathered a large family, many of whom were guides. Captain Pliny Miller arrived in 1822 and in the late 1840s built a small hotel. In 1849, William F. Martin built a hotel on a peninsula in Lower Saranac Lake, a mile from the heart of the village. At that time there were only fifteen scattered families in what is now Saranac Lake, but the hotels began to change that. Martin's Hotel, the first built in the Adirondacks to attract people of leisure and wealth according to Donaldson, attracted everyone visiting the Adirondacks for thirty-one years following its opening, including Adirondack Murray, whose tales began the rush to the mountains. Among the artists who favored Martin's were William J. Stillman and Arthur F. Tait. In 1858, Stillman made the place headquarters for the renowned Philosopher's Camp whose members included Oliver Wendell Holmes, Louis Agassiz, Robert Lowell, and Ralph Waldo Emerson.

Many of the early visitors talked of the health-giving climate of the mountains. The visit of Dr. Edward L. Trudeau in 1876 determined the village's destiny. For seventy years, the Village of Saranac Lake has served as a premier health resort in the treatment of tuberculosis. The health industry here affected the architecture greatly, as a walk around the village will show; *Cure Cottages of Saranac Lake*, by Phil Gallos, puts this in perspective.

Robert Louis Stevenson, suffering from tuberculosis, lived here for one winter. The Stevenson Cottage and other points of interest are highlighted in the walking tour pamphlet, *Historic Saranac Lake*, available from the Chamber of Commerce in the Harrietstown Town Hall, at the corner of Main Street and the Lapan Highway. This intersection is also on the Lake Placid-Tupper Lake Highway at the intersection of NY 3 and NY 86.

Trails near the village are steeped in history, and a newly expanded system of ski trails is being built to encompass some of the traditional routes. The Jackrabbit Trail from Keene Valley to Tupper Lake will have many connecting loops in the Saranac Lake region.

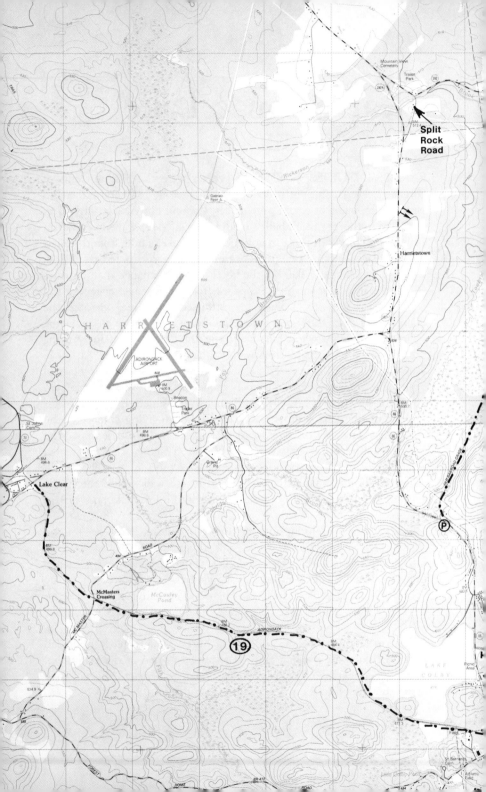

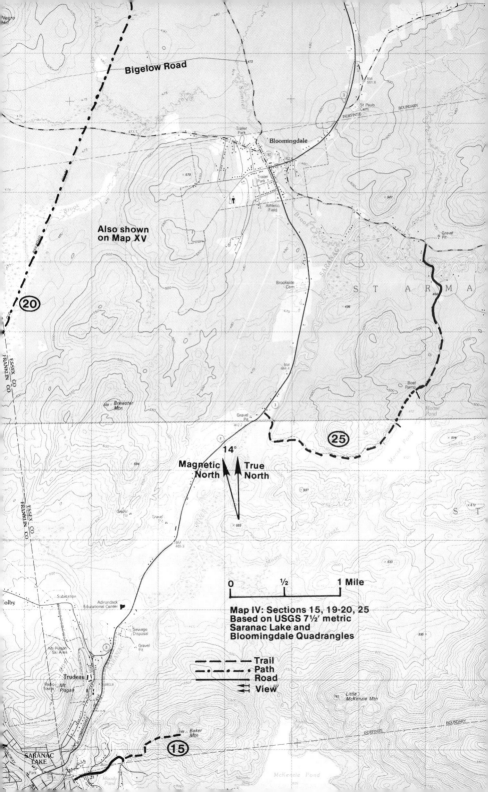

Bigelow Road

Also shown
on Map XV

(20)

ESSEX CO
FRANKLIN CO

Brewster
Mtn

14°

Magnetic
North   True
North

Bloomingdale

Trailer
Park

Trailer
Park

Athletic
Field

Brookside
Cem

Gravel
Pit

St Pauls
Cem

BOUNDARY

INDEFINITE

S T   A R M A

Boat
Ramp

Moose Pond

(25)

0   ½   1 Mile

Map IV: Sections 15, 19-20, 25
Based on USGS 7½′ metric
Saranac Lake and
Bloomingdale Quadrangles

Trail
Path
Road
View

Substation

Adirondack
Educational Center

Sewage
Disposal

Colby

Gravel
Pit

Trudeau

Mt
Pisgah

Little
McKenzie Mtn

SARANAC
LAKE

Baker
Mtn

(15)

McKenzie Pond

INDEFINITE   BOUNDARY

15 Mount Baker

Hiking, snowshoeing
0.9 mile, ¹/₂ hour, 915-foot vertical rise, map IV

Mount Baker is a year-round favorite that offers a great return on a small investment. The round trip, which can be made in under an hour, offers sweeping views of the island-dotted Saranac Lakes, the Village of Saranac Lake, and the High Peaks. The top is studded with ten-inch diameter Scotch pines that offer protection and a musical soughing with any wind; the top-most show sapsucker holes. These trees were planted by Girl Scouts in 1916, a reforestation effort called for by the 1908 fire. Surprisingly, given all the visitors, graffito is at a minimum.

If you start from the Harrietstown Hall, you can walk along village streets for twenty minutes to the trailhead or drive the same route in just a few minutes. Head left up Main Street and bear right past the Hotel Saranac. (The hotel is run by Paul Smith's College as a training ground for its students, and you can stop for early morning doughnuts on the way.) On your left you pass the Saranac Lake Free Library, which houses one of the region's finest Adirondack book collections.

Go straight at the traffic light and continue to a triangle park, resplendent with flowers in summer. Bear right here, just before the railroad tracks. Across the tracks is Stevenson Lake leading to Robert Louis Stevenson's Cottage, which is open to the public. It was here he spent the winter of 1887–1888 and wrote *The Master of Ballantrae*.

You turn right away from Stevenson Lane on Pine Street and in 100 yards turn left on to East Pine, crossing an interesting laminated wood bridge over the tracks. If you are walking, in another ten minutes you will curve to the right around the cattails at the head of Moody Pond to the trailhead on the left, which is marked by a DEC sign. Red disks, perhaps a trifle too sparsely, mark the trail and sort out the confusing paths at the foot of the mountain. An occasional old ADK marker may be seen.

After climbing for about twelve minutes, look for glacial striations on the rock in the trail under your feet. The lower slopes are covered with a rich stand of northern hardwoods, but above 2000 feet, you encounter the plantation of Scotch Pine with a few red pines here and there.

You climb for no more than fifteen minutes when you reach rocks that frustrate snowshoers. The rocks offer a vista to the right of Moody Pond and the Saranacs that is not duplicated at the top.

At the summit, look for two USGS survey markers. Below is McKenzie

Pond and to the left McKenzie Mountain. Oseetah Lake, Kiwassa Lake, the High Peaks—they are all before you. Looking the other way from the summit, a bit east of north, there is an obscured view of the Saranac River. It is worth exploring a bit on the south and southeast of the summit to discover outcrops and openings with views.

16 Harrietstown Ski Trails

12 kilometers in several loops of varying levels of difficulty, map V

The Harrietstown Ski Trails are about a mile west of the village on the road toward Tupper Lake, NY 3. They are a collection of labyrinthian concentric circles for which a map is available at the Chamber Office or in winter at the ski hut at the trailhead. In summer it might be possible to hike these trails, but they can be soggy in places, with the usual complement of mosquitoes. In winter you should wear cross-country skis or snowshoes so you do not punch up the groomed ski tracks.

If you head west from the village, you pass a housing project on the left and also see a log lean-to and a sign for the Harrietstown Ski Trail. To the right is the Trudeau Institute, descended from the famous Trudeau Sanitarium. Turn left, 100 yards to the log hut, the ski center. With a map you can spend several hours exploring these trails, which range from easy skiing to fairly difficult loops for experts. Some trails are lit for nightime use.

17 Lake Placid to Saranac Lake, Whiteface Resort to McKenzie Pond Road

Hiking, skiing
5.5 miles, 2½ hours, 950-foot elevation change, map V

This trail through Forest Preserve land has been incorporated into the Jackrabbit Trail for skiing. It is also an excellent and fairly easy walk. While the trail has a moderate grade as it climbs from Whiteface Resort, there are several steep downgrades as it begins the descent toward McKenzie Pond, giving it at least an intermediate rating. If it is the least bit icy, this trail is for experts only.

This traditional route has been closed to the public for several years because of private land problems near McKenzie Pond on the eastern end. There are currently two endings for the trail, and shortly one of them will become the official one, but thanks to the ski council, access around and through private land has been achieved.

Heading west from Lake Placid, turn north on Whiteface Inn Road at the top of the grade as you leave the village, and drive 1.3 miles to a parking area. The trail, marked also for McKenzie Mountain, heads north of west along an old tote road. (See section 23 for more details of the beginning of this route.) The grade is gentle for 0.5 mile, then moderately steep for the next 0.3 mile. The trail continues climbing gently to pass the lean-to at 1.5 miles and reach the intersection with the McKenzie Mountain Trail from NY 86, section 23 at 1.9 miles.

The trail continues climbing to a height-of-land in a col between Haystack and McKenzie mountains at 2.3 miles. The trail is now all downhill with several steep sections. The trip is gorgeous as the trail passes through mature hardwoods mixed with hemlocks. In several places you have distant winter views. The trail generally follows a stream that drains from the pass or col. The stream, which is not shown on the USGS, is in a fairly deep ravine, and the trail is quite close to it but often as much as seventy feet above it. At about 3 miles, halfway through the steep descent, there is a view back toward McKenzie Mountain and ahead to McKenzie Pond. At 3.8 miles you cross McKenzie Brook, having descended nearly 950 feet from the col.

On the far, west, side of the brook there is a small path leading down to the pond. The trail continues a bit south of west now and comes to an intersection. The way left is a route that has been carelessly hatched out from an overgrown tote road. It leads across McKenzie Brook, crossing it between the pair of marshes that surround it. It approaches the recreation fields, staying just to the north of the ball fields and reaches McKenzie Pond Road at 5.5 miles. The trail straight ahead from the intersection stays on the original tote road for a bit longer before turning south to cross McKenzie Brook through one of its marshes. This route is fine for winter, but might damage the marshes the rest of the year, so even though the trail is now routed this way, the DEC may elect to use the other route. This trail turns west, circles around the recreation area, and reaches McKenzie Pond Road at about 5.4 miles. The blue signs of the Jackrabbit Trail mark the parking area at this end of the trail on McKenzie Pond Road, about halfway between NY 3 in Saranac and NY 86 in Ray Brook.

While this trail was reopened as a ski trail, the beauty of the forest make it especially desirable as a hiking trail. Note that you can use it with section 23 for a long, but attractive approach to McKenzie Mountain from Saranac Lake instead of Lake Placid.

18 McKenzie Pond Road to Saranac Village
Cross-country skiing, map V

West of McKenzie Pond Road, at the end of the McKenzie Pond Trail, section 17, the Jackrabbit Trail follows a tote road south, then curves east through a lovely red pine plantation. It curves west to pick up the Fairytale Railway, the portion of the Delaware and Hudson that runs between Saranac Lake and Lake Placid. The trail follows that railroad into Saranac Lake, where it hooks up with the Harrietstown Ski Trails. At present it leads to the North Country Community College Campus, through Riverside Park, across the highway, and behind the high-rise apartments into the woods to the Harrietstown Ski Trails.

From there, a route will eventually head north past the grounds of the High School and Saranac's recreation fields to join the New York Central Division Railroad bed, section 19.

You could ski the railroad from NY 86 west of Ray Brook where it winds south of Ray Brook and heads east toward Lake Placid. It has been remarked about this portion of the railroad grade that it is so boring, snowmobilers do not even use it.

19 The New York Central Adirondack Division Railroad Bed from Saranac Lake, past Lake Colby, McCauley Pond, McMaster Crossing to Lake Clear Junction
Cross-country skiing, bicycling
5.6 miles, 2½ hours, level, map IV

The abandoned railroad grade crosses Broadway in Saranac Lake and heads west past athletic fields to reach a causeway across Lake Colby at 0.4 mile. The causeway is nearly 0.3 mile long and has lovely views of the lake. Beyond it, the route angles north to wind through a series of marshes

Lycopodia

starting at about 2 miles. McCauley Pond comes into view at 3.5 miles, and you continue along its southern shore, cross its outlet, and reach McMaster Road at 4.3 miles. From here it is 1.3 miles generally north to Lake Clear junction.

One exciting part of this route is the proposed extension along the bed of the Paul Smith's Electrified Railway to Paul Smiths (see that chapter introduction). That extension may be completed before this guide is revised. It will connect with trails around Paul Smiths and at the new Visitors Interpretive Center. From Paul Smiths, the route will head south, following some of the trails described in this guide, and gradually wind its way to Tupper Lake. Those who want the challenge of a long trail should inquire locally for updates on the Jackrabbit Trail.

20 Bloomingdale Bog
Path along an abandoned railway, maps IV and XV

The Chateaugay Division of the Delaware and Hudson Railroad reached Saranac Lake from Plattsburgh in 1887. Its route north of Saranac Lake made use of level stretches along sand flats and beside bogs that border Twobridge and Negro brooks. These wandering brooks are the only open water in the bogs, which represent a late stage in bog transition, for much of the area is relatively dry. In the south, the Bloomingdale Bog is filled with acid-loving shrubs such as leatherleaf that grow in clumps and mounds rising out of the sphagnum base. Cranberries and pale rhododendron also thrive on these hummocks that are distinctive of such an advanced stage bog, underlain with sand. Grass pinks, rose pogonia, and other orchids are secreted in the hummocks.

Farther north near Negro Brook, the soil is still acid, but the sand flats, where the water is very near the surface, support huge black spruce and tamarack. Under the pines and balsams on the dryer borders you find an unusual range of lycopodia, lichens, and mosses. Serviceberry and cherries are filling the open marshes. Early settlers drained portions of these bogs to grow vegetables.

Parts of the northern end of Bloomingdale Bog are Forest Preserve, and other parts have been acquired by The Nature Conservancy. The state hopes to acquire much of the rest in the near future. The railroad grade makes an excellent nature walk and introduces you to a variety of plants. In winter, the route is an excellent ski trail. Several roads cross the railroad so it is easy to explore more than 5 miles of this unusual corridor.

North of Saranac Lake, 1.3 miles beyond the hospital, where NY 86 starts to bend west, turn right down a one-lane, unnamed, narrow dirt track, heading north. This leads to private but unposted land in the wettest part of Bloomingdale Bog where the tracks, marked as a snowmobile trail, are like a boardwalk into this special place.

A northern access is a west turn from Oregon Plains Road opposite Swinyer Road, which leads east to Vermontville. Oregon Plains Road leads north from Bloomingdale. The west turn, Merrill Road, is a dirt road that crosses Negro Brook and shortly beyond reaches the railroad grade, along which you can walk either north or south. Not all the bridges over stream crossings survive, however. To the south, the railroad crosses Bigelow Road, but a better access is from NY 192 between Gabriels and Bloomingdale. Here the railroad, along which you could drive, leads south into Bloomingdale Bog itself. The 4-mile stretch to NY 86 north of the hospital may be the best and easiest nature walk in the area. In places it is dry enough to leave the railroad bed to explore; in others, you will get wet if you try it.

Driving between these four access points, be sure you head west on NY 192 to Split Rock Road and look at the enormous split erratic in the field beside the road. You often see bluebirds here as well. Turn south on 192A to NY 86, toward Saranac, and watch as you pass the Harrietstown Cemetery. There are lovely views across the Bloomingdale Bog with a panorama of the High Peaks beyond.

McKenzie Wilderness Area

NORTH OF SARANAC Lake and Lake Placid lies one of the Adirondack's smaller Wilderness Areas. Records of how much of it was logged are impossible to find. In 1917, International Paper Company, which owned a large part of the area, began lumbering operations on the eastern slopes of its mountains. Donations of the Shore Owners Association of Lake Placid and others made it possible for the state to acquire the land for the Forest Preserve before IP could log it.

The Shore Owners Association was founded in 1893 in order to acquire the outlet of Lake Placid and regulate the dam. Up to this time, fluctuations in the water level, caused by drawdowns by mill owners along the outlet, had aggravated the shore owners.

In years past, there were many more miles of marked trails along the shores of Lake Placid and to the Wilderness Area's peaks than at present. The Shore Owner's Association of Lake Placid used to maintain trails along the shores of the lake and to McKenzie (Saddleback) and Moose (St. Armand) mountains. Moose Mountain, at 3899 feet, ties with Snowy for honors as the highest peak outside the traditional High Peaks-Dix-Giant areas.

Currently the region offers two good trails to McKenzie Mountain, a trail to Haystack, several level routes, and a wealth of bushwhacks, two of which are covered in the chapter on Ray Brook.

21 Haystack from NY 86

Hiking
3.3 miles, 2 hours, 1238-foot vertical rise, map V

A large parking turnout on the north side of NY 86, 1.6 miles east of the DEC office in Ray Brook, marks the new trailhead to Haystack and McKenzie. This new, blue-marked, longer route that serves as the

McKenzie Mountain summit

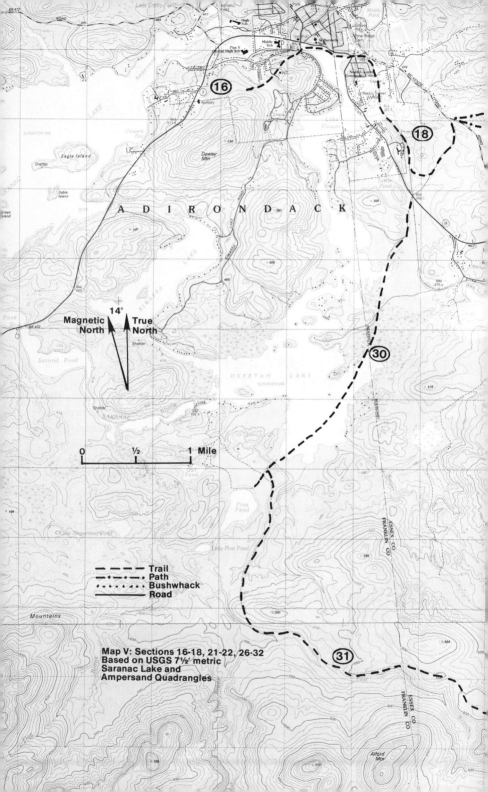

Map V: Sections 16-18, 21-22, 26-32
Based on USGS 7½' metric
Saranac Lake and
Ampersand Quadrangles

beginning of both the Haystack and southern McKenzie trails avoids private land, but it adds a mile to the old route, while adding little interest.

No matter, this is the best way to Haystack and a climb up that sharp little cone is most rewarding. The trail begins in a plantation, curving east of north for 0.5 mile to cross a stream. The trail now bends west-northwest, climbs slightly to a height-of-land, but generally maintains a level contour. It is close enough to the highway so its sounds will reach you. The trail, on bedrock with many erratics beside it, is narrow, but more than adequately marked. At 1.5 miles, after a forty-five-minute walk, a boardwalk leads you across a seep and around the side of a hill. Shortly after, at 1.8 miles, your route intersects the old trail, which is now a wide route. A gradual uphill on the wide trail follows the valley of Little Ray Brook. You approach Little Ray Brook and a minute later cross it on a bridge. At 2.3 miles, the stream splits, and shortly beyond the trail splits. A guide board points ahead 2.9 miles to McKenzie, 3.2 miles east to the Whiteface Inn, and left, the way you turn, for 0.9 mile to Haystack.

You cross a new bridge over the tributary, then hop rocks below a dam in a water system. Then you start right up! There is a brief respite after ten minutes, then the steep pitches resume. You may spot old, red markers here as well as the new blue ones. The trail crosses a series of pitches and shelves, heading generally north. You reach a rock outcrop for a needed rest after a thirty-minute climb. From it you have views of Lake Oseetah, Ampersand Mountain, Ray Brook, and the prison. You can already see Scarface, the Sewards, Donaldson, Emmons, Ouluska Pass, Panther, Giant, the Great Range, Marcy, MacIntyre, and Colden.

Another ten minutes will take you to the summit. Below the rock patch on Haystack's southern summit, you see Big Burn Mountain, Lake Placid, the Sentinel Range, Pitchoff, Cascade and Porter, the long slope to Railroad Notch, First Brother, Big Slide, Basin, Saddleback, Armstrong, and Gothics. Through a notch in the Range you can see to Dix and the Beckhorn. Marcy and Haystack (the High Peak) are to the left of it then Little Haystack. From Marcy and Grey, you can sweep right to Colden, Avalanche Pass, Wright, Algonquin, Boundary, Iroquois, Indian Pass, the back of Wallface, Street and Nye, MacNaughton, Donaldson, Emmons, Seward and Seymour, and Ouluska Pass. Quite a view for such a tiny mountain.

An interesting variation on this hike is a short bushwhack descent to the northeast, 60° true, to the high pass on the trail from Whiteface Resorts to McKenzie Pond, section 17. The bushwhack is about 0.4 mile long and the descent is about 180 feet. A right, east, turn on the trail takes you

Lake Placid from McKenzie Mountain

downhill in 0.4 mile to the McKenzie Trail, sections 22 and 23. Turn right again, south for 1.2 miles to the intersection where you started up Haystack. This bushwhack is much longer, but with much gentler grades than the direct descent south from Haystack. Hikers who want to climb both Haystack and McKenzie in one day often use this bushwhack route as the shortest connector with the McKenzie Mountain Trail.

22 McKenzie from NY 86

Hiking
5.3 miles, 3 hours, 2221-foot vertical rise, map V

At the turnout to Haystack, at 2.4 miles, section 21, stay straight on the wide old trail now marked with red. It continues beside Little Ray Brook, climbing more noticeably. The trail crosses two small streams 100 yards apart at about 2.6 miles and a third stream at 3.4 miles. Beyond the trail is quite eroded and often very wet.

At 3.6 miles, you reach an intersection. The way right is the trail of section 23, where the rest of the route to McKenzie is described. This steep, just over 1.6-mile, stretch accounts for 1440 feet of the climb up McKenzie.

23   McKenzie Loop from Lake Placid

Hiking, spectacular views
8 miles, 7 hours, 1940-foot ascent, map III

This loop makes use of two trails, the DEC yellow trail for the ascent, one of the Shore Owners Association of Lake Placid trails for the descent. To find the joint trailhead, go west from Lake Placid on NY 86 to the top of the grade as you leave the center of the village and turn north on Whiteface Inn Road for 1.3 miles. Here, on the left, there is an old logging road. The town road ends 200 yards beyond near new condominiums.

There is a "Jack Rabbit Trail—Welcome" sign at the barrier 65 feet up the logging road. Further on a short distance, at the state boundary just beyond a trail to the right marked "Powder Run," there is a DEC yellow trail sign with distances listed for Placid Lean-to, Haystack and McKenzie Mountains, and NY 86. Follow the road up the slope for 0.3 mile until it levels off. The forest changes from old-growth beech, birch, and maple to mixed second growth with conifers. At 1.5 miles, the new Placid Lean-to sits up on a small rise on the north side of the trail.

At 1.9 miles there is a junction in the trail; a sign points south 3.6 miles to NY 86 at Ray Brook and 2.1 miles to Haystack, sections 21 and 22. Straight ahead, west, leads in 2.5 miles to McKenzie Pond, section 17. The way right is the 1.6-mile trail to McKenzie Mountain that you will follow. It is level only briefly, then very quickly heads steeply up the shoulder of McKenzie. As the slopes steepen, paper birch crown the rock outcrops. The only difficult part of the trail is here and it is slow going. At 2.6 miles, you have climbed 800 feet to a ridge. There is an opening with views on the south side of the trail. The climb is more gentle now, through spruce and fir with a lovely ferny understory, along the narrow ridge and over a minor summit, about 2.8 miles, then a second, at 3 miles, and a third, at 3.2 miles each with limited vistas.

About three hours out, after a sharp descent and an even sharper ascent from a col, you are finally on top of the highest part of the ridge, at just short of 3.6 miles. Paths lead 50 feet to either side. To the right, east, you see views of the high country, from left to right, Whiteface towering over the horizon, Gothics, the Great Range, Marcy, and all around to the Seward Range. To the left, you see Saranac Lake, and going to the north, the Saranac River Valley, Franklin and Union Falls, Catamount in the northeast, and a distant skyline of Azure, Debar, and Lyon mountains. There is a panorama of high country and the Park's northern boundary.

Here at the summit you have three alternatives, to retrace your steps, to descend to Bartlett Pond, right below to the southeast, and continue back to Lake Placid via the minimally maintained and signed SOA Trail, or to bushwhack 2.5 miles along the ridge to Moose Mountain. Unfortunately the old trails that headed toward Moose are long gone, and even the bushwhack proves to be almost impossible. An alternate bushwhack is suggested in section 24.

To head toward Bartlett Pond, continue following the trail, along the ridge, starting down in 100 yards. You drop down into a saddle where there are two old signs; one indicates the overgrown Catsworth Trail to St. Armand (Moose) Mountain. You descend along a gradual traverse for about twenty minutes to the north end of Bartlett Pond, 4.3 miles. Walk right around it to its outlet where the SOA trail heads downstream on the far side of Two Brooks. You are above, then close to the brook. Thirty minutes from the pond there is another old sign, indicating Saddleback Mountain (referring to McKenzie's double summit) 2 miles. Shortly, at 5.6 miles, another sign reads "Twin Brooks Trail to St. Armand Mtn. (Moose)," but there is little evidence of it. (Nor is there any indication why the stream was called Twin then, and Two Brooks on the current USGS map.)

The last 0.6 mile to Lake Placid is a lovely forest walk under mature yellow birch, sugar maple, and red spruce. You are following the brook and come to the foundation of an old reservoir dam. The trail pulls away from the brook and joins the SOA trail at 6.2 miles at a sign indicating the lake trail and the Twin Brook Trail, 1.5 miles, to Bartlett Pond, which you have just descended. Continue along the shore to the Whiteface Resort where signs warn you that you are crossing at the owner's pleasure. The town road, with no signs, is just ahead and leads to your parked vehicle at just short of 7 miles.

24   Moose Mountain
Bushwhack, map III

Although Colvin visited McKenzie Mountain in 1878, early in his triangulation work, he did not even mention Moose until his report of 1895. Today, the only way to get to the summit of Moose Mountain is via a long, seven-hour, bushwhack of over 4 miles round trip, plus a short, 1.3-mile, forty-minute walk along a trail on either end of the bushwhack. Start at the Whiteface Resort Road and walk along the SOA Trail to the Moose Mountain Trail, reversing the end of section 23. Walk up the trail for about 0.6 mile to the old Moose Mountain (Saddleback) Trail that has disappeared. Turn north here on a faint herd path, all that remains of the trail, and walk through mixed hardwoods, on a course about halfway between true and magnetic north. The going is easy, with a steady ascent. Keep the general compass heading, but stay with the herd path which is not hard to follow at first. Surveyors' tapes, one within sight at almost all times, make the job easier.

At about 3100 feet elevation, after a 1 $^2/_3$-hour bushwhack of 1.5 miles if you have been able to follow a fairly straight route, you begin a slight descent to a stream, which is the headwaters of Two Brooks. You cross and recross the drainage a few times, then you should spot a path crossing the stream, heading away from it and up a fairly sharp hill, which is the beginning of the main cone of Moose. It is 0.5 mile and an 800-foot climb from the stream valley to the summit. About a third of the way up from the crossing, the going gets rough, as you are now out of hardwoods and into blowdown. Keep checking your compass heading if there is any doubt about the path. As long as you keep climbing and keep your heading you will not miss the summit, as there are no false summits or ridges.

Near the top there is a narrowing, a sort of channel, which will pop you out between the east and west summit domes. You will want to check out views from both. On the return, look for the path as you come out of the blowdown; it will definitely shorten your trip. Blowdowns are heaviest if you veer to the west before the stream crossing. From the stream to the summit takes 1$^1/_3$ hours, almost that long for the return. However, from the stream crossing down to the SOA Trail takes no more than an hour.

25   Moose Pond

Easy trail, fishing, camping, hiking, cross-country skiing
1.5 miles, 40 minutes, relatively level, map IV

Moose Pond is a gem secreted to the north of the McKenzie Range; from its western shores there are lovely views of that range. There are two accesses to it. For both you drive north from Saranac Lake along NY 3, where you have good views of the McKenzie Range above the marshes that surround the Saranac River. NY 3 makes a sharp right turn in Bloomingdale. Beyond the turn, 0.15 mile, take another right, this time onto River Road (the sign points to Franklin Falls.) Turn right again 1.65 miles along River Road. There is no sign, but this is Moose Pond Road. In

View across Moose Pond to the McKenzie Wilderness

0.4 mile it crosses the Saranac River and at 0.85 mile it reaches the end of winter plowing. From here you can ski the 0.7 mile along the rolling road to the boat launch on the north shore of Moose Pond. In summer you drive the last 0.7 mile and start walking along the informal path that leads south along the west shore to lovely promontories. In winter, if the lake is securely frozen, ski out on it to get the best views of the McKenzie Range.

Many fisherman and campers use the boat launch site. Campers paddle to lovely sites on promontories above the lake. Fishermen vie for the lake trout for which the pond is famous. The state stocks the pond, keeping fishing good. Although there are paths along the western shore, it and some of the points on the eastern shore are all too accessible by boat. Rocks on these points glitter with browns and greens, not unusual minerals but broken glass.

The second access to the pond is a trail for hiking that is especially good for skiing and avoids the most heavily used areas. It leaves from NY 3 between Bloomingdale and Saranac Lake. The beginning, not conspicuous at all, is 4.3 miles north of Hotel Saranac in the Village. There is no trailhead parking area, just roadside parking beside a field. Look to the east along a fence that crosses the field. About 100 yards from the road, a narrow hiking bridge over the Saranac River is marked with DEC trail signs at the beginning of the trail.

The trail follows an old woods road with a canopy of second growth trees and the grade never exceeds 50 feet in elevation change. Across the bridge you turn right to follow the river for 50 feet or so, then head along a fairly level contour to the lake. The way is pleasant and easy through a beautiful woods setting. This is a trail for anyone.

The trail winds around a small mountain through a forest of small balsam fir and the pioneering hardwoods: aspen and paper and yellow birch. Interspersed is a mix of ash, black cherry, red spruce, occasional white pine and hemlock, and lots of northern white cedar. The forest cover indicates that although the area was logged, it was never cleared extensively. The white cedar, more prevalent by the pond, occur along the trail. Their presence indicates a high water table and shallow soils over rock ledges. And ledges there are. In a dozen or more places little outcrops border the trail. They are capped with white cedar and in winter festooned with icicles stained with yellow and brown.

The road approaches the lake and follows the shore about 200 feet back from it. A third of the way up the shore, the trail peters out. Years ago, several homes stood near here, in fact at one time, quite a development was planned for the shores of the lake. Ski tracks will lead you downhill to a beautiful site on the shore with an old chimney. Just beyond is a rocky bluff, a picturesque spot from which to view the lake. To the east you see Whiteface and Esther, while in the mid-ground stands Slide Mountain. To the right and very close, Moose and McKenzie thrust wooded slopes skyward. You can ski along the lake shore, visiting promontories that in summer are easy to reach by canoe. Moose Pond is a gem in a wilderness setting, close to the highway in miles, but far away from civilization.

Near Ray Brook

A GROUP OF mountains rise both north and south of NY 86 near Ray Brook in the town of North Elba between Saranac Lake and Lake Placid. South of the highway 3088-foot Scarface with its sheer rock face dominates views from the highway. To the east lies 2484-foot Seymour, whose summit offers views out of proportion to its diminished height. To the north, on the southeastern fringe of the McKenzie Range, stands a cluster of small mountains; and every day thousands of people whizz by on NY 86 without realizing how much interesting territory awaits tramping just beyond the salt-scorched trees lining this most heavily traveled of Adirondack roads.

The northern cluster consists of Big Burn, Little Burn, Little John, and Hennessy mountains with Little Burn and Hennessy being the smallest and closest to the highway. Hennessy rises directly behind the clearing, which was once the Sara-Placid Drive-In Theater. Little Burn, situated behind the Mountain Paper Company building, can be viewed well from the Saranac Lake Golf Course across the street.

In the early years of this century, the golf course was Meadow Brook Farm, the first scientifically operated dairy farm in the region; but, long before that, it was part of the Daniel Ames farm. Daniel Ames was one of the earliest settlers in the Ray Brook Valley. His farm was the site of one of the two sources of iron ore (the other was Cascade Lakes) for Archibald MacIntyre's Elba Iron Works, established on the Chubb River in 1810. The Ames ore pit was probably somewhere between the highway and the foot of Little Burn. The Ames house (not the original homestead) is a white Greek Revival building just west of Mountain Paper on the north side of the road. It is very likely the oldest domestic structure in the Saranac Lake-Lake Placid area.

26 Scarface Mountain

Hiking
3.2 miles, 2 hours, 1480-foot vertical rise, map V

The first 1.5 miles of this route is a new trail. This section was rerouted in 1981 when a federal correction facility was built nearby. There is a good-

Scarface Mountain

sized parking area at the trailhead. Just west of DEC headquarters on NY 86 in Ray Brook, turn south on Ray Brook Road. The trailhead is 0.1 mile down the road.

This new trail makes for a delightful walk through a hemlock and white pine grove. The route is marked with red disks. In five minutes you cross the Fairytale Railroad tracks. This is now an abandoned railroad right-of-way that runs between Remsen and Lake Placid.

In another five minutes or so you can see on the right the pond into which Ray Brook flows. Shortly, at 0.5 mile, you cross the brook in an alder swamp. The rather impressive bridge proclaims its history with a wooden plaque: "This Bridge Built October 1981 By Camp Adirondack Crew #5, Rebuilt By Camp Gabriels August 1985, Crew #3."

At the far end of the bridge, a staircase takes you back into the woods. Another five minutes sees you in an open meadow with blueberry bushes. There is a surprising number of flowers in the mature forest that follows— pyrola, wood sorrel, hawkweed, sheep laurel, to mention some. The trail continues fairly level, heading southwest.

When you arrive at the old trail at 1.5 miles, you bear left. This is a tote road that is narrowing down to trail width in places. In five minutes, at

1.75 miles, you take a left off the tote road onto a narrow trail through a mixed forest. You follow a brook for ten minutes. Occasionally, there are beat-up ADK markers.

Now climbing, the trail leaves the brook at about 2.2 miles. It is mostly deciduous forest, which becomes predominantly birch as it approaches the summit. It is surprising to see a number of large, healthy beech trees.

You have a moderate climb in a southerly direction most of the way. There is one steep pitch shortly before the first open ledge, which, at just short of 3 miles, faces west to north. You can see Ampersand Mountain, Lower Saranac Lake, Oseetah Lake, and the village of Saranac Lake. A herd path left leads to a lookout north toward Whiteface.

In two minutes, you arrive at the next open ledge. Facing southeast to northwest, the view is lovely—Street and Nye, MacNaughton, and the Sawtooth Range, with Couchsachraga behind the first and second and the Sewards behind the fourth, Ampersand Mountain, and Oseetah Lake. From here, you enter the woods and in five minutes reach the summit. There is a small open area with limited views. The two open ledges that you reach first a bit below are the spots to linger and enjoy the scene.

This is an excellent mountain for hiking. It offers diversity along the trail, as well as unusual perspectives of other mountains from the summit area.

27 Little Burn

Bushwhack, map V

Access to Little Burn and Hennessy is easiest via the new (1984) DEC trail to McKenzie. The trailhead is on the north side of NY 86 at a point 1.6 miles east of DEC headquarters in Ray Brook. An excellent loop trip consists of a mile walk along this trail, a climb of Little Burn, a long traverse to Hennessy, and a descent from Hennessy along a brook, back to where the trail crosses the brook, about 0.5 mile from the highway. Begin by following the DEC McKenzie Mountain Trail. At 0.5 mile you cross a brook that comes from the northeast. This is where you will intersect the trail when you descend Hennessy. Continue on the trail and as you approach a height-of-land at about 1 mile, watch for low ledges that line the north side of the trail.

Leave the trail, following a compass bearing of 10° over the ledges and up the slope beyond. For the next 125 yards, steep pitches alternate with easy to moderate breaks. Then the grade becomes steep to very steep with numerous big rocks scattered about.

At a sequence of steep ledges, 165 yards from the trail, turn left and follow the base of the ledges on easy grades to a group of large boulders at the bottom of a shallow draw that breaks through the ledges and provides a route upward. You are now about 205 yards above the trail. Bear right into the draw, climbing at first moderately, then steeply and very steeply among rocks until the way ahead becomes boxed by ledges and boulders at 240 yards. There should be a cliff to your right.

Turn right and head on fairly level ground to the bottom of the cliff at 255 yards. Turn left and work your way up around its base along a game path at moderate to steep grades to a group of boulders at 290 yards. Turn acutely right, heading 75° and ascending at a moderate grade to the top of a rock knob at 340 yards. There are views of Cascade Mountain in the southeast to Long Pond Mountain in the west.

From a spruce tree at the top of this knob, head toward magnetic north on level ground, then at 370 yards, climb moderately and steeply up to the ledges and cliffs at 390 yards. Turn left and follow the base of the ledges, mostly on the level, to 410 yards where they can be climbed. Bear right and go up over the ledges, heading more or less magnetic north on moderate grades to 450 yards. Now make a very acute right turn and scramble up onto the south rim of the western spur of Little Burn Mountain. Follow the rim eastward over easy grades on open rock to the summit of the spur, just above a large erratic boulder at 560 yards.

The views from the south rim range from Hennessy Mountain nearby to the east around to Mount Baker to the west, but the entire scene is dominated by Scarface Mountain just about due south across the Ray Brook Valley. Scarface conveniently divides the vista into two nearly equal but strikingly different segments.

To the left of Scarface are the High Peaks, including, from right to left: Santanoni, MacNaughton, Street, Nye (with its 1983 earthquake slide), Saddleback, Gothics, Armstrong, Big Slide, Cascade, and Pitchoff. Nearer at hand, about in line with Marcy, is the diminutive Seymour—not the 4120-foot peak most people associate with that name.

To the right of Scarface is the Saranac Intramontane Basin, a 35-mile-long, 15-mile-wide valley containing 150 lakes and ponds. Some of the basin's lakes are visible as are many of their surrounding mountains. From left to right, you can see Seward, Alfred, VanDoren, Ampersand, and Stoney Creek mountains, Mount Morris, Lake Oseetah and the Saranac River with Wolf Pond in the foreground, Boot Bay Mountain, Floodwood

Mountain, Shingle Bay Mountain, Lake Flower, Long Pond Mountain, Saranac Lake Village, and St. Regis Mountain.

The north rim of Little Burn offers still another view. From the summit, follow 325° compass bearing 48 yards to a small open ledge. Big Burn Mountain looms almost menacingly large to the north. Left of it are the Haystack of Ray Brook, Little McKenzie Mountain, McKenzie Pond, Mount Baker, and the western portion of the view you had from the south rim.

Your elevation on the spur is 2300 feet. Hiking time is about one hour to this point. The true summit of Little Burn, on a hump to the east, is 30 feet higher, but there is not much to be seen from it; so, from here you might as well go directly to Hennessy.

28 Little Burn to Hennessy
Bushwhack, map V

Beginning from the summit of the spur, section 27, follow the spur's crest easterly over easy ups and downs for 140 yards. Then you begin a moderate descent to the bottom of a saddle that you reach in 185 yards. Someone has blazed a trail with surveyor's flagging, and your route from the top of the spur has coincided with it up to this point. Here, though, the flags march off northward, presumably to loop back east onto the top of Little Burn proper. You should turn right, go out of the saddle, and then maintain your elevation by traversing the south slope of Little Burn while heading easterly.

The crest of the ridge will be above you to your left (north). At its east end, it noses off with ledges at 565 yards. From here, follow a compass bearing of 100° for the next half mile, pretty much aiming yourself at the northernmost and highest of Hennessy's four summits.

At 865 yards, you encounter the first of a series of small streams and watercourses flowing from the north. All are headwater runs of what Phil Gallos calls Ames Brook—the brook you crossed on the McKenzie Trail 0.5 mile from the highway. A second, slightly larger stream, is encountered at 915 yards. There is a rocky drainage to cross at 955 yards; and, at 990 yards, there is another small stream. Here, also, you re-encounter and cross the flagging. You cross a wet area with multiple drainages from 1025 to 1060 yards.

Elevation change has been insignificant since you began following the 100° heading; but now you begin a gradual ascent to Hennessy Brook, a

tributary of Ames Brook, which you will intersect at an acute angle at 1240 yards. It will be flowing from your left. Hold to your course, crossing the brook and climbing at easy and moderate grades to ledges topped with spruce and fir at 1430 yards.

Now turn right. Work your way up along the base of the ledges at moderate grades until the ledges break down at 1445 yards. Turn left and begin a very steep climb up through spruce growth with a few scrambles over mossy ledges on the spine of Hennessy's north summit. The grade begins to moderate at 1515 yards. Continue following the spine in spruces at moderate to moderately steep grades until you come out upon the lower, west, end of southwest-facing ledges at 1540 yards. Here there are views from south to northwest. Climb moderately steeply another 20 yards to the highest point on these ledges. The view includes the High Peaks from Marcy to Santanoni, as well as a westward vista from Ampersand to Long Pond Mountain in the distance with Little and Big Burn at right foreground.

From here, follow the spine east on the level and down a bit to a southeast facing ledge—really the brink of a small cliff—at 1635 yards. The view here sweeps from the Sentinel Range (east) to the Sawtooth Range (south). Cobble Hill, much of Lake Placid Village, and, when the trees are leafless, parts of Lake Placid Lake, can also be seen.

Your elevation is 2530 feet, 230 feet higher than the spur of Little Burn, though the views are not as extensive. The sense of seclusion, however, is greater because this summit of Hennessy (unlike its southernmost summit) is considerably farther back from NY 86. Allow about an hour to get here from Little Burn.

29 Descending Hennessy

Bushwhack, map V

Reverse the route described to climb Hennessy directly or combine it with sections 27 and 28 for a loop to this summit and Little Burn. In order to return to the McKenzie Trail from the viewpoint on Hennessy, head west for a few yards to a break in the ledges and descend steeply 35 yards into a saddle between your summit and the next one to the south. There seem to be two classes of inter-summit saddles: those that give an impression of shelter and calm in an otherwise stormy place and those that seem to be

Ampersand Mountain and Lake Oseetah from Little Burn

funnels for the wind, wild and chaotic. This saddle is one of the peaceful ones.

Turn right and follow a compass heading of 300° out of the saddle at easy grades, which become moderate at 120 yards and moderately steep at 160 yards. The grade begins to slacken at 235 yards, gradually becoming easy once again.

At about 310 yards, you come to Hennessy Brook. Follow it downstream, left, at easy to moderate grades. The stream breaks up now and then and at times is quite ill-defined, making it especially challenging to trace in winter. At 625 yards, Hennessy Brook joins Ames Brook at the head of a ravine. Ames Brook comes in from the right. Follow it downstream, staying high on the right, north, bank to avoid rough going in the ravine. The grades are still moderate and easy.

If you poke about in an old clearing, which you reach at 885 yards, you find the disintegrating remains of a lumber or freight wagon, parts of an old iron stove, some crude stonework, a few apple trees. Who was here? It is unknown. But, whoever they were, they must have been here after 1908 because the forest fire that swept these slopes that year would have obliterated the wagon and killed the fruit trees.

From the clearing, you can descend the rest of the way to the McKenzie Trail on an old tote road that is fairly easy to follow in most places. It parallels Ames Brook, so even if you lose the road, you will not lose your way. At 1100 yards, you reach the trail where it crosses the brook. Turn left. You have half a mile to walk to the highway for a total loop distance of just under 3.5 miles and a total trip time of just about three hours, not counting your stops.

30 Oseetah Lake to Pine Pond

Cross-country skiing
3.3 miles, 1½ hours, level, map V

Oseetah Lake, a many-fingered widening of the Saranac River, has a number of summer cottages and private homes. It also has a wild eastern shore with miles of marshes pierced by an esker and a number of cedar-, pine-, and birch-topped rock islands, which dot the lake as well as the marshes. A wonderful snowmobile trail leads to the lake, across the marshes, and around the southern bays of the lake to reenter the woods and head toward Pine Pond or toward the circuit of Scarface Mountain that ends at Averyville Road, section 31. Most of the time the trail is on the lake; it is well away from the lake's developed shores.

Views from the expanse of marshes and water are of the scarred face of Scarface, west to Ampersand, and south to the Sawtooth Mountains and the northern slopes of the High Peaks, and north to the McKenzie Range. Out on the lake you can pick out Baker, McKenzie, Haystack, Moose, Whiteface, Seymour, the Sentinels, Scarface, Colden, the Sawtooth Range, the Sewards, and Ampersand. The trail leads through the marshes that are filled with leatherleaf, cranberries, and reeds. Beyond the marshes, a rich border of evergreens curtains the lowlands. Whether you ski the marshes and the lake, or make the much longer circuit to Averyville Road, this is a superb ski trail.

Note that you can also reach Pine Pond in summer by canoeing from the boat launch in Saranac Lake Village up the Saranac River, south through Oseetah Lake—a winding trip around its many islands—and across the open expanse of Oseetah Lake to the southern bay and trailhead for Pine Pond. The trail from Oseetah to Pine Pond is only 0.4 mile long. Pine Pond is a kettle pond, the depression left by a melting chunk of glacial ice. The sand accumulated at the edge of the pond makes it a great place to swim. The sandy shores support stands of pine, what else? All this makes Pine Pond a delightful destination in both summer and winter.

One Saranac Lake Chamber of Commerce ski brochure describes a slightly different route for the ski trip than the one given in this guide. Oseetah Lake is a greatly enlarged version of the original Miller Pond. Flooded now are huge expanses of marsh, and the lake encompasses parts of the Saranac River, which can move quite a bit of water beneath the ice. There is often open water along the river's course, so this guide's approach is safer.

In winter, the trail begins from the south side of NY 86 at Fowler's Crossing, the parking turnout where NY 86 crosses the Fairytale Railroad, 1.7 miles west of the DEC office in Ray Brook. The sign says 1.1 miles to Oseetah Lake, but what this means is unclear. The trail heads south through a red pine plantation that gives way to white pines at about 0.5 mile where the trail splits. The right fork approaches the lake to the west and continues on to village roads along Lake Flower. If you turn this way, you reach the lake at 0.7 mile and can wind west and south around the islands to the Pine Pond Trailhead.

It is better to take the left fork, the trail, that continues downhill slightly to the marsh and cranberry bogs and across them to open water at 0.8 mile. From here on there are no markers to guide you—only the tracks of

Oseetah Lake Marsh

snowmobiles made by those who know the best route. You continue generally south, across more of the marsh to cross a road at 1.2 miles. This private road leads from Ray Brook across a causeway in the marshes to homes on the esker/peninsula. The trail now leads southwest through the marshes, passes between two of the rock islands, and out to the frozen surface of the lake. From here you continue southwest, along the southern side of a chain of islands, heading toward a tiny island. Continue along this route, southwest, siting past the island to the far western corner of the south lobe of the lake. Here at about 2.9 miles from the start, you find the trail to Pine Pond. The bay that approaches the trail is narrowed by marsh grasses and shrubs, but the beginning of the trail is marked and obvious.

The trail heads southwest for 0.15 mile to a fork. Stay right for Pine Pond. On your return you can explore the bays and islands to the north of the lake. Note, however, that where the river flows swiftly in the channel beside islands and in the pass at the northern end, there is usually open water. If there is any question, return as you headed out.

31 Oseetah Lake to Averyville Road
Cross-country skiing, Map V
10 miles, 5 hours, moderate grades

This route is currently marked as a snowmobile trail and it is well used. Unfortunately, the land at the eastern end, at the end of Averyville Road, is private. This was the old trailhead for the northern part of the Northville-Placid Trail; private land problems have caused that trail to be rerouted to farther north along Averyville Road. Parking and access from the end of Averyville Road is permitted during the winter months for snowmobiles and cross-country skiing. This is an exceptionally handsome ski trip that can be skied one way in either direction if transportation is provided at each trailhead. In fact, if you plan to ski this route one way rather than round trip, beginning at Fowlers Crossing on NY 86 may be preferable to the direction described.

Follow section 30 to the beginning of the Pine Pond Trail on Oseetah Lake and head southwest along that trail for 0.15 mile to the fork. Turn left and continue generally south. You can see Pine Pond through the mixed red and white pine forest. You pass two paths leading to the pond. The trail rises gently uphill, south, then arcs southeast to approach Cold Brook at about 2 miles in a lovely stand of hemlock.

The next 2 miles or so are a gradual uphill to a height-of-land with one hairpin turn in the stretch. You pass several side paths leading north to Rogers Brook; one leads to the site of an old hunting camp. At 5.2 miles there is a right fork that leads 0.25 mile south to a beaver dam on Cold Brook, a good place to visit and turn around if access through to the northeast is not possible. The trail now swings north, climbing over the shoulder of a small hill. At 6.4 miles you pass the intersection with the old Northville-Placid Trail. This is about the end of state land. The forest of conifers is open enough for views of Street and Nye, with the new slide on Nye most prominent. A road forks north to Cameras Pond near the parking area located at the end of the town road at the westerly edge of a large potato field.

32 Seymour Mountain
Bushwhack, map V

There are not as many Seymour Mountains in the Adirondack Park as there are Owls Heads, but there is at least more than one. The Seymour most people know is the 4120-foot High Peak east of the Seward Range; the Seymour between Lake Placid and Ray Brook is a much smaller version.

Standing just east of Scarface Mountain, overlooking Alford Pond and the settlement of Averyville, this modest mountain is not really connected with anything. Though it seems close to settled places, it is in an odd way isolated—isolated by its very nearness to peopled lands. The logical route of ascent would involve crossing the fields of Averyville and climbing the mountain from the shore of Alford Pond. It is the simplest, most direct way, and there is even a path up from the pond. The problem is that there is over 0.5 mile of private property between Averyville Road and Seymour Mountain. Those easily crossed fields, that convenient path, are not open to the public.

None of the other ways of climbing Seymour through state lands—four separate routes were checked—were easy. Interesting, but not easy. However, the views from the summit and especially from a big southwest ledge are much more than simply interesting.

This route involves a woods road, railroad tracks, a path, and 1.3 miles of bushwhacking, the kind that presents an orienteering challenge with 0.9 mile on a single heading through a mature forest on nearly level ground.

Hiking begins from the south side of NY 86 where a woods road starts at a barred gate 1.8 miles east of DEC Headquarters in Ray Brook. Follow the woods road for 0.55 mile through the Clifford Pettis Memorial Forest. The grades are mostly easy and mostly downhill.

C. R. Pettis is a major figure in the history of American forestry. He was appointed New York Superintendent of Forests in 1910, and a year later he established the first state nursery at Saranac Inn. The system of nursery practice that he developed there was adopted by the U. S. Forest Service and was taught at all forestry schools. The forest you are now walking through was once scorched earth, a boneyard of trees left by the fire of 1908, reclaimed by Pettis' pine seedlings from Saranac Inn.

The road ends at a railroad and powerline right-of-way. Cross the tracks, turn left, and walk easterly beside the rails a short way. Just before the first power pole in this direction, a path climbs the embankment to your right. Follow the path. About 150 yards from the end of the woods road, the path turns right. As it descends into the forest it becomes a more obvious trail.

Cross a muddy spot and 100 yards farther arrive at a bridge over the east branch of Ray Brook. The path comes to the west branch of Ray Brook in another 70 yards and parallels it closely, upstream along its right bank until crossing it on another bridge in 180 yards. At this point you are 0.3 mile from the end of the woods road, 0.8 mile into the walk. The nearly level section between the two bridges is quite pretty, especially along the West Branch.

After crossing the second bridge, the path briefly climbs steeply and then rises and falls gently through a mixed hardwood and hemlock forest well away from the brook. The path is wide and very straight because it is the route for an underground pipeline that brought water to the old Ray Brook tuberculosis sanatorium, now the New York State Department of Corrections Camp Adirondack, 2.5 miles to the west.

You encounter the brook again at 1 mile and recross it on a third bridge 70 yards farther along. Then the path climbs moderately with a few steeper pitches up through an exquisite ravine in which the brook tumbles over clusters of boulders and cascades down long, steep slabs of ledge rock at the base of the northeast spur of Scarface Mountain. If you do not have time for a longer trip, this ravine is a worthy destination in itself.

The grade eases at the top of the ravine at 1.2 miles, and you reach a small dam in another 100 yards. The pool behind the dam is the water source for the pipeline that runs under the trail.

At this point, 1.3 miles, bushwhacking begins. Follow a compass bearing of 110° from true north, 125° magnetic, and ascend a steep band through evergreens. You reach the top of the bank about 50 yards from the dam. Now continue following the same bearing through mature hardwood/ spruce forest, mostly on the level with some very gentle ups and downs. You are heading straight for the mountain, but you will not be able to see it, even in winter when the leaves are down. There is a fairly substantial amount of detritus on the forest floor, sometimes thick with witchhopple, and occasional clumps of young spruce. These factors make walking in a straight line nearly impossible, so frequent reference to your compass is essential. You may come very close to a slope that drops moderately to steeply away to the left. Avoid descending it if you actually intersect it. Instead, follow its rim to a predetermined reference point along your bearing and then resume your original course.

Eventually, the plateau-like area you have been crossing will begin to slope upward more noticeably. The land narrows between the drop-off to your left and a hill on your right. Stay on the shelf between them until you reach a small stream (it may be dry) at 2.2 miles, after 0.9 mile of bushwhacking. Turn right and walk upstream nearly into the saddle between the hill and Seymour Mountain itself. Turn left and ascend Seymour. The grades vary from moderate to very steep. You can best avoid the cliffs and unclimbable ledges by staying on a line north of the summit. If you do this, your 500-yard climb should bring you into a large draw that leads you to a sag on the crest of the mountain, just north of the summit outcrop at about 2.5 miles.

The nature of the topography atop Seymour makes attaining the summit a tricky business, especially in winter. From your position in the sag, you are faced to the south with a vertical rock wall. The best thing to do is work your way up around its right, west, flank, finally reaching the summit from the southwest after a 250-yard scramble. Your elevation is 2484 feet, and you have come 2.65 miles from NY 86 in about two and a half hours.

Though the highest bit of rock is completely in the open, the view is punctuated by the spirey tops of spruce and fir trees growing up from lower levels. The trees are like window frames through which you can look at scenes from the Sentinel Range around to Nye and Street mountains. There is also a little window toward Whiteface. The best views, however, are from a wide ledge at the top of a southwest-facing cliff not far below the summit. Finding the ledge is a matter of simply leaving the summit in a southwesterly direction and poking around until you come to open rock verging on a major drop—no trees in front of you.

From this ledge, there is a wonderful panorama from Big Slide Mountain and the High Peaks clear around to Mount Baker and the base of the McKenzie Range, about 190°, with the roundish sheet of Alford Pond and the fields of Averyville at your feet. Scarface dominates the view westward, and there are two very interesting prospects to either side of it. One, to the southwest, reveals the southernmost of the High Peaks—Santanoni and Panther—through a deep notch between Street Mountain and the Sawtooth Range. The other is an unusual view down the Ray Brook Valley toward Saranac Lake village, the lake country, and St. Regis Mountain. This was the route of the first road, begun before 1810, to link the western lake basins with the river valleys east of the High Peaks. Today it is still a major corridor for travel and settlement.

Between Saranac Lake and Tupper Lake

THE SARANAC AND Raquette Rivers and the Indian Carry between them were the principal means of travel between Saranac and Tupper lakes in the nineteenth century. The present highway linking the villages on these two lakes was not built until 1888.

Before that, Tupper Lake had a few hotels for sports from the big cities and several small mills. Accessible lumber from the region was floated down the Raquette, but no good roads led to markets.

The Tupper Lake region held vast quantities of timber, enough to convince John Hurd that an extension of his Northern Adirondack Railroad was a wise investment. The road was begun in 1883 and reached Tupper Lake in 1889, by which time 75 million board feet of logs had been harvested and stacked along the railroad right-of-way, waiting to be taken north to mills near Malone. More important from a forest fire point of view was the fact that no attempt was made to clean up on both sides of the tracks for miles. One of the early travelers on the line remarked that on both sides of the track for miles, piles of dead branches and logs and overturned stumps gave look of devastation to the forest that before the railroad was "glorious country, a primeval forest undisturbed in all its native grandeur."

The village of Tupper Lake became a frontier town, the largest producer of lumber in the state. Hurd's sawmill, built on the shores of Raquette Pond, was said to be the largest sawmill ever erected in the state. From seventeen families in 1889, the population of the town leaped to 1051 individuals in just two years.

A second railroad reached the town only two years after the first: Dr. William Seward Webb built a competing line from Remsen to Malone, connecting Tupper to the south as well as the north, and allowing trains to go from New York City to Montreal using this route.

Succeeding mills made pulp as well as sawn logs. The Santa Clara Lumber Co. brought logs from the slopes of Seward and Ampersand mountains and the Cold River region.

All this was jeopardized by a fire in July of 1899 that destroyed 169 buildings, almost all of the settlement at Tupper Lake. The town rebuilt

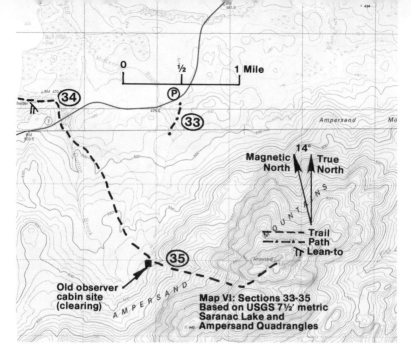

Map VI: Sections 33-35
Based on USGS 7½′ metric
Saranac Lake and
Ampersand Quadrangles

along its modern lines, and logging and lumber products remain a major source of income for its residents.

This chapter includes several trails accessible from the highway between Saranac and Tupper Lake, among them routes on the south side of the highway that seem to fit better here than in the projected High Peaks guide since they are physically isolated from that region. Included also is one bushwhack south of Tupper Lake, which is in a parcel of Forest Preserve east of NY 30, and isolated by lands held by various lumber or paper companies. This seems the only place to describe this orphan mountain that lies so far south of the logical boundary of this guide.

33 Hemlocks

Path, nature walk, map VI

A proud stand of hemlocks, up to over eight feet in circumference, offers a chance to experience the feel of an old-time virgin forest.

Drive west for 7.2 miles from the Town Hall in Saranac on NY 3, toward Tupper Lake. Park at the second turnout or parking area on the right, north, side and cross the road into the trees on the south side. If you are coming east from Tupper Lake this spot is 8.1 miles from the "Y" junction of NY 3 and 30 at Wawbeek.

The stand is almost all hemlock, with little ground cover except club moss and ferns. The unmarked footpath is easily visible, unless obscured by snow. The tall trees offer a cool walk in hot weather; look for pink lady's slippers in late spring.

After following the path for ten minutes, you will in one step cross a small stream whose banks are guarded by grey birches. Such an extraordinary variety of mosses can be found on the rocks in the stream and on the bark of trees near this crossing that it is a place where botanists stop to study them.

For another ten minutes you walk beneath the stately hemlock with occasional spruce, birch, or white cedar. Then, as you walk into the "U" bend of a stream, the hemlocks begin to thin and the trail branches into confusing fingers. Across the stream are a few more big trees, but the best is behind you. The temptation is to follow the "U" around to your left and inscribe a nice circle back to the start, but the path becomes difficult to follow and skirts the hemlocks on the return, so your best bet is to turn around and retrace your steps. Getting lost in this grove is deceptively easy, and once away from the road noise, the wind in the trees sounds like traffic. And, when you are lost, the look-alike hemlocks do not seem so friendly.

The path you are following used to go to hunting camps and led past an extensive bog. With the removal of the camps, the path can no longer be followed this far.

34 Middle Saranac

Trail, nature walk, picnicking, cross-country skiing
0.5 mile, 20 minutes, level, map VI

A large parking lot on NY 3 serves as Ampersand Mountain's Trailhead. It is 8.3 miles west of Saranac Lake and 7.1 miles east of the intersection of NY 3 and 30 at Wawbeek. A short trail heads north from this lot to the shores of Middle Saranac Lake and a lovely sandy beach and picnic area. The trail generally follows the west banks of Dutton Brook.

At the lake there is a lean-to and a wooded swamp at the southwest edge of the beach. If you walk north along the beach past another swamp, you will find an esker that supports a stand of pure red pine. These native trees like to face the wind along the lakeshore, and they thrive in the fine sands and shallow soils of the esker.

35 Ampersand Mountain

Hiking
2.8 miles one way, 2 hours, 1790-foot vertical rise, map VI

Ampersand Mountain sits apart from the High Peaks in the Ampersand Primitive Area. They are separated by a corridor of private land. The mountain's isolation gives it wonderful views of the High Peaks and it is often considered one of those noble heights. Its trail begins on the south side of the road, opposite the parking area, see section 34. The trail, defined with red DEC trail markers, offers a lovely, more or less level walk for 1 mile, through a mixed forest—stately hemlock, maple, birch, and beech. The beech are small; most of the large ones have died out.

As you start out, you reach a long plank walkway over a wet, muddy stretch in ten minutes or so. In another three minutes, you cross Dutton Brook on a log bridge, set corduroy style.

This easy part of the walk gives you a chance to warm up for the fairly steep climb to the summit area. The grade gradually increases and after a steep pitch where the trail circles around under slopes at the head of a sharp little gully, you reach a small clearing at 1.4 miles. This is the site of the fire observer's cabin. The old trail crossed McKenna Brook here before continuing partly on stairs for the precipitous climb toward the summit. The current trail makes a sharp right turn, southeast toward the brook and follows it heading steeply up the mountain. The mile-long climb covers a thousand feet and takes the better part of an hour. You will use your hands to pull yourself up a few of the steep pitches. The trail is eroded and often presents a sheer wall of mud, but it is usually obvious in spite of the fact hikers try to stray from the trail to find a better route. Most of the time the spruce that cling to the slopes are too dense to allow much straying.

The trail levels off in a draw, then angles north toward the summit. The final approach to the summit is gorgeous. To your left are massive rocks; a huge split rock on the right invites exploring. Enough people have left the trail here to explore the rocks and crevices that you will find a number of small herd paths. If you are leading a group of young people, be sure they do not stray too far.

Soon the rock walls are rising on both sides of the trail. In the last 0.3 mile you climb over 300 feet to the open rock summit. Your way is marked with yellow paint blazes, pointing the easiest way to the eastern end of the summit. Although it is all open rock, many small evergreen bushes and

Ampersand Summit

flowers cling to the niches. On a rock wall in a cleft near the summit is a memorial plaque: "In Loving Memory of Walter Channing Rice, 1852–1924, 'Hermit of Ampersand,' Who Kept Vigil From This Peak 1915–1923, Erected by His Sons, 1930."

Rice was a guide, then an innkeeper at Saranac Lake who returned to guiding after the death of his wife. He spent eight years as a fire observer on the mountain top, gaining a reputation for his homespun philosophy and his love of nature.

The only trace of the steel fire tower that was erected here in 1921 (replacing an earlier, 1911, wooden tower) are bits of shattered glass and the four metal posts that anchored it. The fire tower was located beyond the highest point of this mountain.

No tower is needed for the magnificent 360° view. Ampersand's location on the border between mountain country and lake country makes this vantage point one of the best views in the Adirondacks. To the south, from east to west, you see the Sawtooth Range, the Sewards, and Long Lake. Many lakes range north. Facing east, you see Scarface nearby. Leading on around to the north, you see Whiteface and the McKenzie Range.

The summit, however, was originally totally wooded and owes its open rock to Colvin who had his men cut lines from the summit toward his other signal peaks in 1873. Fires and erosion bared the rest.

Leaving the summit, be sure to walk east past the draw to pick up the trail where it enters the woods. Notice that you will leave the summit heading south, even though the trailhead is to the northwest. As soon as you reach the rock walled area, there should be no further questions of direction, so just follow the markers and the foot tread.

36   Weller Pond to Saginaw Bay on Upper Saranac Lake

Short walk accessible only by boat, cross-country skiing
1 mile, ½ hour, 180-foot elevation change, map VII

This short trail traverses a ridge between Upper Saranac Lake and Weller Pond and serves as a canoe carry between Middle and Upper Saranac lakes. Magnificent forest cover, solitude, and quiet are its attractions. You can make a one-day outing by canoe to picnic on the shore near the trailhead and return. Either carry your canoe along the trail to Middle

Saranac that follows Dutton Brook, section 34, or, much easier, put in 1.65 miles to the west along NY 3 at South Creek boat launch, which is just to the west of the bridge. From the boat launch, paddle into Middle Saranac and north into its northern bay, called Hungry Bay. The mountain to the east of north is Boot Bay Mountain.

It is a little over 2 miles to the northeast corner of Hungry Bay and the outlet of Weller Pond. Canoe up the outlet, and northwest across Weller Pond to the trailhead at the far end of the pond. One of the prettiest parts of the 3.5-mile canoe trip is the short section along the outlet of Weller Pond; bog plants including pitcher plants and sundew grow in sphagnum mats beside the waterway.

The trail heads generally north, climbing the ridge. It is well marked and easy walking, especially if you are not carrying a canoe. While all of the destinations in the Saranac Lakes are quite popular, this walk remains a remote treat.

Weller Pond is a delightful ski destination in itself. The preferred route is down the trail to Middle Saranac, section 34, then northwest across the lake. As you emerge from the woods to the lake, you can quickly tell if winds are so strong as to make skiing on the lake unpleasant. From the lake there are good views of Whiteface, McKenzie, and Ampersand mountains and south to the Sewards. Your course takes you toward Halfway Island and if you go between it and Umbrella Point, your course takes you close to Windy and Reben Points. The latter was named for Martha Reben, whose tuberculosis brought her to the region. Her stay at a campsite in Weller Pond as well as a later one at Reben Point effected something of a cure. She survived to write three inspirational books, all filled with the beauty of the surrounding mountains.

From Reben Point, head north through Hungry Bay and the channel and on to Weller Pond as described above.

37 Panther Mountain

Trail, views
0.7 mile one way, one hour round trip, 500-foot vertical rise, map VII

This short, somewhat steep trail provides a pleasant view of the Raquette River Valley for a relative minimum of effort. The trailhead sign is located on NY 3, 1.6 miles from its intersection with NY 30 at Wawbeek Corners.

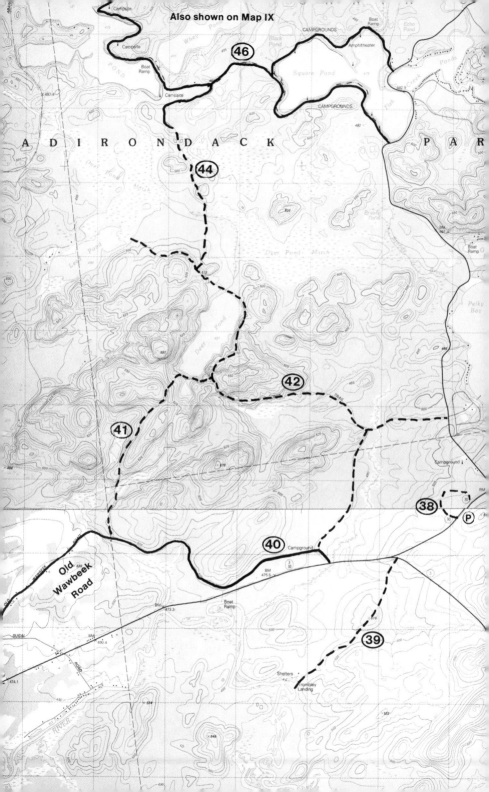

Also shown on Map IX

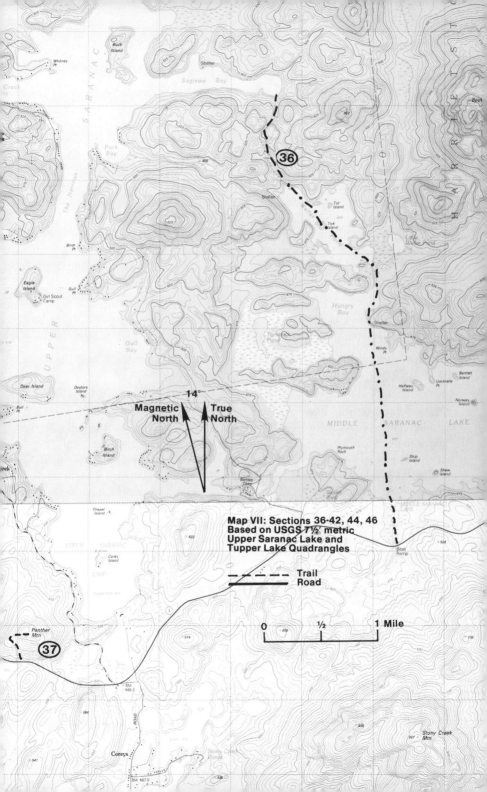

Map VII: Sections 36-42, 44, 46
Based on USGS 7½ metric
Upper Saranac Lake and
Tupper Lake Quadrangles

Trail
Road

0   ½   1 Mile

14°

Magnetic
North

True
North

36

37

Drive toward Saranac Lake until you see the parking lot on the right; the trailhead is immediately opposite on the left.

The sign states it is 0.8 mile to the top of Panther Mountain, but it is actually somewhat shorter than this. The climb is a steady progression through different forest types. Beyond the conifers of the lower slopes, and the maples and beech of the mid-slopes, birch of the upper slopes finally give way to the grassy bald summit. This summit was burned over late in the last century, and the shallow soils and strong winds have prevented the forest from recolonizing up to the present time.

On the top, there is a metal disc of the USGS. Chimney stacks of the old paper mills at Tupper Lake are visible on the western horizon. Tiny Panther Pond lies to the south beneath its namesake mountain while beyond are good views of Ampersand and the Seward Range.

38 Fernow Nature Trail
Interpretive trail, cross-country skiing
1.2 miles round trip, 40 minutes, level, map VII

A short distance from Wawbeek Corners lies one of the relatively few self-guided nature trails in the Forest Preserve. Named after one of the early pioneers in American forestry, Bernard Fernow, this trail is a mixture of native hardwoods with an almost mature conifer plantation.

The trail begins at a parking area on the west side of NY 30, 0.75 mile north of the intersection of NY 3 and 30. It starts under a canopy of native beech, sugar maple, and yellow birch. After a few minutes you reach a trail register where you can usually obtain a booklet describing the nature trail.

The trail itself is a mix of the natural and the historical. Imposing specimens of white pine and Norway spruce are identified as well as remnants of the prior hardwood forest that re-sprouted at the stump. Various glacial erratics are noted. The booklet indicates general principles of modern forestry.

Red squirrels have been present since the forest first returned to the area after the passing of the glacier and the tundra that followed it. Not so the Norway spruce upon which the squirrels feed today. Conifers were considerably more valuable than hardwoods in the nineteenth century, so Fernow clear-cut the original hardwood forest and then burned the resultant slash and residue to form a better seedbed for the spruce. This act was not appreciated by influential camp owners on nearby Upper Saranac Lake, and they used their influence to prevail upon the state legislature to fire Fernow from his position as head of the College of Forestry at Cornell; and indeed, forced the closing of the college itself. The college subsequently reopened in 1911 at its present location in Syracuse, and the experimental station was moved from nearby Axton on the bank of the Raquette River to its modern site at Newcomb.

This short trip through a slice of Adirondack history, both cultural and natural, is somewhat longer than the distance indicated on the sign.

39 Trombley Landing

Cross-country skiing, fishing, canoeing, hiking
1.6 miles, 1 hour, relatively level, map VII

A pleasant 3.2-mile jaunt in and out along an old truck trail takes you to a pleasant spot on the Raquette River with two lean-tos and primitive campsites. The trail, named after an early woodsman of the area, descends a gentle grade to arrive at its destination. The route is a great short ski trek. Use it also for a short walk to a lovely picnic site.

Trail access is from a recessed, gated trailhead at the southeast corner of the intersection of NY 30 and 3, Wawbeek Corners. The trail, marked with yellow disks, crosses a creek at 0.3 mile, where the grassy glade is filled with Joe Pye weed and mosquitos in August. The whole area shows signs of the early century burns, for the forest cover ranges from pole-sized hardwoods to pioneer stands of aspen, white birch, and black cherry, to extensive scotch pine plantations.

After a leisurely walk or ski, you reach the landing where the Raquette River meanders through a wide flood plain with abundant silver maple. Upriver lies Axton, the site of the State Forestry School when it was under the auspices of Cornell University. Here a canoe launch site is accessible from the road past Coreys, on a road that heads south from NY 3, 2.5 miles east of Wawbeek Corners. Downriver is the DEC boat launch site on NY 30, 1.5 miles west of the Corners, and farther downriver still is the Village of Tupper Lake, where canoes may also be launched on the Raquette north of the bridge over the river. Between these points, and for quite a way upriver from Axton, the Raquette is a slow flowing, meandering river that invites leisurely exploration.

40   Deer Pond Cross-country Ski Loop

Hiking, cross-country skiing
7.3 miles, 4 hours, undulating, map VII

The state has recently designated the eastern end of Old Wawbeek Road as the trailhead for a 7.3-mile cross-country ski loop to Deer Pond. There is parking for several cars along the plowed first hundred yards of the road, which is 0.6 mile west of the intersection of NY 3 and 30 at Wawbeek Corners. Parts of the loop make excellent hiking trails and are described in greater detail.

The loop begins by heading west from along Old Wawbeek Road, paralleling NY 30 for about a mile, then heading northwest to reach the end of the plowed section of Old Wawbeek Road at 2.4 miles. In summer you can reach this point by driving along Old Wawbeek Road or approaching from the west as section 41 describes.

From here the loop follows the trail of section 41 as far as Deer Pond, then turns east on the trail of section 42 at 4.3 miles, 1.9 miles from Old Wawbeek Road. The loop continues east on that trail for 1.5 miles to turn south on an old roadway at 5.8 miles. From here it is a clear route along an old road for return to the parking area at 7.3 miles.

41   Lead Pond Trail from Old Wawbeek Road

Marked snowmobile trail, cross-country skiing, hiking, fishing
3.9 miles, 2 hours, undulating, map VII

This well-marked trail leads to a little frequented pond at the edge of Forest Preserve land south of the campgrounds. The trail passes two other lakes as it makes its way in an up-and-down course, ascending and descending a number of ridges on its way to its destination. Overall relief change, however, is minimal.

Turn north on Old Wawbeek Road from NY 3 and 30 just east of the Sunmount Development Center on the western edge of Tupper Lake Village. Drive northeast on Old Wawbeek Road for 2.4 miles and park carefully on the roadside. The trail heads north.

After walking approximately ten minutes through a thick plantation of exotic European spruce, you begin to descend to a lushly verdant beaver pond. The profusion of vegetation present in full sunlight here is in stark contrast to the barren understory of the heavily shaded conifer plantation. A beaver pond nestled in the forest like this is an ideal habitat for wood ducks and hooded mergansers.

You cross another ridge before the trail dips once again to skirt the shores of Mosquito Pond. Only half the open area here is actually open water, the other half consists of low heath and marsh plants so typical of bogs in general. Breeding pairs of ring-neck duck have been seen here during mating season.

Leaving Mosquito Pond, at 0.9 mile, about half an hour walk, the trail begins to ascend another ridge—this one crowned with a magnificent stand of mature beech and sugar maple. A drop in the trail takes you to the shores of Deer Pond. Just beyond, at 1.9 miles, there is a trail junction. The trail coming in on the right is the Deer Pond Trail, section 42, that starts on the truck trail on NY 30. Bear left, but leave the trail heading downhill to a nice place to have a picnic lunch on the shelf rock overlooking the lake at this point. The encircling ridges and the usual solitude prevailing here impart a sense of peacefulness.

The trail now rises again to yet another ridge, leaving behind the splendid specimens of yellow birch and hemlock on the lakeshore. After a short stay on the ridge the trail gradually descends to an extensive boreal wetland at 2.9 miles and continues through that wetland all the way to Lead Pond. At 3.2 miles, the trail from Rollins Pond Campground, section 44, comes in on the right. One more mile of mostly level walking and you are at the boggy shores of Lead Pond, 3.9 miles from your start.

The east end of the pond is in the Forest Preserve, the west end is private.

42 Deer Pond Trail

Cross-country skiing, hiking
2.4 miles, 1¼ hours, undulating, map VII

This marked ski trail, which begins on a former DEC truck trail, leads to a fairly large interior lake that receives heavy use in spring and early summer by fishermen. At most other times of the year, you will probably enjoy the handsome mature forest traversed by this trail in complete solitude.

The trail's beginning is at a point 1.8 miles north of the NY 30 and 3 intersection at Wawbeek Corners. A gated truck trail on the west side of the highway is the start of the trail. The guide board gives the distance to

NY 3 and 30 via Deer Pond as 6.6 miles and part of this trail is incorporated in the loop of section 40.

You begin by walking for ten minutes along a shady aisle through an almost mature plantation of exotic Norway spruce with some native white pine. Then you come out into a large open wetland where beaver have been active recently. The forest is relatively open after the wetland. A sandy glacial outwash supports stands of immature red spruce and balsam fir.

At 0.8 mile, you reach an intersection with the ski trail that leads 1.4 miles south to the Deer Pond Cross-country Ski Area Trailhead.

The two routes become one and continue through the dense thicket of conifers that flank their route. This is optimum breeding habitat for many boreal birds, and in springtime the mating song of the ruby-crowned kinglet chimes through the stillness.

The trail now ascends a ridge adorned with tall sugar maple and beech. In early spring, before the deciduous trees leaf out, a valley can be seen distinctly on the left, lying at the foot of a ridge that is parallel to the one you are traveling on. The physiography of the upland areas of the Saranac Lake Wild Forest is broken here into a series of alternating ridges and valleys of bedrock. As the trail approaches the top of the ridge, a bare outcrop appears on the right, just before the junction of the trail with the marked snowmobile trail from Old Wawbeek Road, section 3. At this point you have traveled approximately 2.3 miles from NY 30.

All along the trail, if you look carefully, you will be surprised at the hair-filled scats of the eastern coyote. Canids also like to travel along these secluded trails, unlike the deer who stay off them.

From the intersection, it is 0.1 mile downslope to the shores of Deer Pond. A shelving rock over the water here provides a nice place for a picnic. A ridge on the far side of the pond is crimson tinted in spring with flowering red maples trees, and it is ablaze in scarlet in autumn when these same trees put on their fall foliage festival.

43   Coney Mountain and Litchfield Hill
Bushwhacks, historic trips, map VIII

A traveler on NY 30 between Long and Tupper lakes crosses a historic boundary line. In 1772, surveyor Archibald Campbell laid out the north

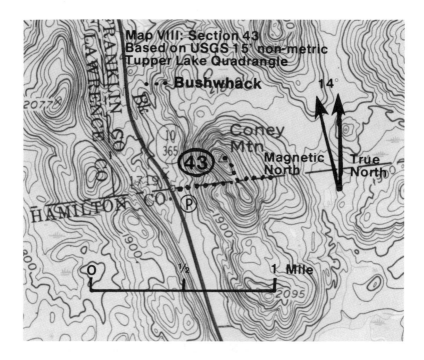

Map VIII: Section 43
Based on USGS 15' non-metric
Tupper Lake Quadrangle

line of the Totten and Crossfield Purchase. He was accompanied by a delegation from the Indian tribe from which the vast tract was being purchased. About 0.3 mile east of today's NY 30, they intersected the north end of the "Line of Mile Trees," which had recently been run 55 miles from the "Landing House Tree House" on the Hudson River.

Beyond this junction Campbell did not continue his line, but he did take his Indian companions up to the shoulder of Coney Mountain where they could look east to the High Peaks and be satisfied that the line was correct.

In 1796, after the American Revolutionary War, Campbell's line was used as the south line of the Macomb Purchase; for this, Medad Mitchell continued the original T & C line east of the Coney Mountain terminus. It was not until 1799 that Benjamin Wright, later chief engineer for the old Erie Canal, carried the T & C/ Macomb line all the way to the Old Military Tract as today's Preston Ponds.

Over the succeeding century, there were numerous property line problems with the original line, but it was finally verified by a resurvey, which is covered in detail in the *Reports of the State Engineer and Surveyor* for 1903 and 1904. Along this 50-mile line there are now almost 300 I-beam monuments and innumerable paint blazes. The south line of St. Lawrence and Franklin counties, and the corresponding north boundaries of Herkimer and Hamilton counties, are coincident with the T & C/ Macomb line.

The present trip to Coney Mountain begins where the county line crosses NY 30, a highway that did not exist until approved by the voters in 1918. This is not a difficult trip, but it requires an experienced eye and a constantly alert mind.

There is a grassy parking space off the highway. Stand a few feet north of the county sign on the west side of the road, and look east between the signs to a utility pole, with its transformer, at the top of the high cut bank on the east side; you are looking along the Totten and Crossfield line.

Before setting out, make a right-about-face and walk about 100 feet west just into the woods. There you should find one of the steel I-beams (#156) of the 1903 survey, daubed with red and yellow surveyor's paint and surrounded by paint-blazed witness trees. Yellow paint blazes will be helpful companions during the day's trip.

Now climb the east bank and enter the woods behind the utility pole. Follow the occasional yellow blazes and the faint hunter's path up the steady slope, detouring around blowdowns and tangles as necessary. Each time, the yellow blazes will put you back on track. On the south side of the blazed line is private Sperry Ponds property.

Just as you see the grade steepen ahead, you will come to the I-beam #158 at the junction with the above mentioned Line of Mile Trees. This is where Campbell's measurements ended. Climb steeply to the top of Coney Mountain's shoulder and hunt for the low I-beam #159. This is also the point at which the rum was supposed to have run out so the survey party wanted to go no farther. Attempts to verify this apocryphal part of the story have yielded no results, yet.

Now begins the scenic part of your day. Turn north, left, and descend into a saddle, following slightly below the top of the shoulder on its east side. At the northwest corner of the saddle, resume your northward climb. Soon you will come to a lookout where the MacIntyre Range is visible far to the east. It seems very likely that Campbell made this slight detour in order to show his Indians the view eastward. His field notes do not contradict this interpretation. (At I-beam #159 on the shoulder, the views eastward and westward are obscured, and in 1903 the surveyors had to make substantial cuttings for their sight lines.)

After this view, it is possible to pick your way along bare rock to the summit where there is a full 360° view. Clockwise from Tupper Lake on the north, the principal landmarks are nearby Litchfield (Goodman) Mountain, Coney's twin; Mount Morris; the Sewards, the MacIntyres, and Marcy; and Santanoni, Blue Mountain, and several lakes and ponds to the west. At your feet you will find three USGS benchmarks and some eyebolts.

To round out your historical day, you may want to return to I-beam #159 and follow the yellow blazes east along the Mitchell/Wright portion of the line. It is easier to start your descent to the south of the I-beam. Almost to the foot of the gradual east slope you will come to Monument #160, a double I-beam at a tri-county corner with its associated witness items. This is the southwest corner of the Macomb Great Lot #1 (and the southeast corner of Great Lot #2) and the southwest corner of the Litchfield Tract. It was also the original Franklin/St. Lawrence/Hamilton corner, but this has since been moved about 0.7 mile west, beyond NY 30.

Just before you reached I-beam #160, you may notice as you cross an abandoned tote road a 15-foot birch stub at the east edge of the road. This may well be Medad Mitchell's corner tree of 1796 for the south end of the Macomb Great Lot #1 and 2 boundary.

East of the I-beam #160 the location of the county line was disputed by Litchfield who had surveyors of the 1903 resurvey arrested for trespassing. Ultimately the location of the Campbell/Mitchell/Wright line was sustained, but the land east of #160 remains private.

This mountain was not always called "Coney." During the century between Campbell and Colvin, it acquired the name "Peaked." During the Colvin surveys, it was incorporated into the triangulation network as the key to the nearby Franklin/St. Lawrence/Hamilton county-corner, becoming "Monument Mountain" in the survey records.

LITCHFIELD HILL

This short (1 mile) bushwhack lacks Coney's history, but not its views. The small mountain is quite obvious from NY 30 and the views to the east from its summit are really stunning. Below lies the stone castle of Litchfield Park, whose construction seems more fitting of the Rhine Valley than the Adirondacks. The lands of Litchfield Park remain privately owned; in the 1920s they were devoted to the preservation of the region's wild game as well as imported animals. The Adirondacks' first (and only?) wild boar hunt was held within the confines of this game preserve.

Litchfield Hill itself lies on state land just to the north of Coney. The bushwhack begins on the eastern side of NY 30, 0.4 mile south of the intersection of County Route 421. Here a wide roadway (once an access road for Litchfield Park) begins at a spot known as Lumberjack Spring. The spring is to the right and is still used by residents of Tupper Lake.

An unmarked path following the old road rises gradually until at 0.6 mile you see a distinct shoulder-ridge of the mountain ahead and to your left. Walk directly north up the spine of the hill to the summit at 0.9 mile.

Several open, clifflike areas on the hill are fairly inaccessible and the view of Tupper Lake to the north and west is blocked by trees. But the views to the east are ample reward for such a short trek. Return by retracing the ridge back to old Litchfield Road. The hill is sometimes called Goodman Hill, after a family that for many generations owned the historic stone out at the foot of Bog River and who recently conveyed almost all of the surrounding land to the state via the Nature Conservancy.

Fish Creek and Rollins Pond Campgrounds

A NUMBER OF trails of varied topography and vegetative cover in the Saranac Lake Wild Forest can be explored from a base at the Fish Creek Pond and Rollins Pond campgrounds, two separate but interconnected state campgrounds that are among the most popular in the entire park. With 622 mostly waterfront sites, they receive heavy use during the summer months. Indeed, it has been said that many city dwellers have been introduced to the Adirondacks through these campgrounds, and they certainly offer an excellent base for probing trails in the surrounding area. But, because of the crowds, trails emanating from the campground are best explored before Memorial Day or after Labor Day. Hiking in late April and early May before the black flies lets you also enjoy early spring flowers. Winter is wonderful for skiing, and most water surfaces are frozen from January through March. If you want to camp in summer, advance reservations are necessary. Floodwood Road and the Mohawk-Malone Railroad form the northern boundary of the wild forest, and the ponds south of that line are full of motorboats in summer.

Despite this intensive use, much of the intrinsic natural beauty remains, especially during the off-season. The campsites themselves are surrounded by handsome forests, and the entire area is one of numerous enchanting glacial ponds, many of them interconnected by waterways. Their shores are usually rimmed by stands of mature conifers and graceful white birch. A park road connects the two campgrounds. Two loops that begin at the campgrounds make circuits of many charming, glacial scoured ponds, no two of which appear exactly the same. Colored in a rich palette of deep blues, greens, and turquoises, to reflect their depth, clarity, and mineral content, the waters of these ponds differ noticeably from the typical Adirondack pond with their tannin and bog-iron-stained shades of brown. Whether it is the color of the water or the types of mature forest that frame the ponds, the ever-changing vistas are fascinating.

The entrance to Fish Creek Campground is from NY 30 just over 5 miles north of the Wawbeek Corners intersection of NY 3 and 30. Campground roads surrounding Fish and Square Ponds continue west to Rollins Pond and its campsites.

44 Lead Pond from Rollins Pond Campground

Cross-country skiing, marked trail, open wetlands
3.4 miles round trip, 2 hours, relatively level, maps VII and IX

This trail starts on the paved park road that links Fish Creek Pond Campground with Rollins Pond Campground at a point 4.0 miles from the gate at Fish Creek Pond. A sandy woods road forks left here and is the beginning of the trail. It leads under a towering canopy of native white pine, which thrive on the glacial sandy soils prevalent here.

Shortly, on the left, you see a boreal wetland well strewn with evergreen heaths. The trail then begins a slow descent to pass through an extensive low-lying area with swamp conifers in abundance. You cross one large creek, the outlet of Deer Pond Marsh, at 1.5 miles. As of the summer of 1987 the way was clear here, but occasionally beaver can be a nuisance along this trail. After crossing the low-lying area, the trail begins a slow ascent up a hardwood ridge dominated by medium-sized maples and beech with some birch.

Finally at 2.1 miles, the trail intersects with the main red-marked Lead Pond Trail, section 41, coming from Old Wawbeek Road. You turn right here and follow the main trail another mile to Lead Pond. After enjoying the boreal second growth forest around the pond, you retrace your steps back to the campsite road, or, alternatively, to Old Wawbeek Road or NY 30 if you have spotted a second vehicle at either trailhead, sections 42 and 43.

45 Floodwood Loop

Snowmobile trail, cross-country skiing, fishing, hiking
7.7 miles, 4 hours, undulating, map IX

Floodwood Loop begins and ends at Fish Creek Campground, following two different north-south routes that are connected by a portion of Floodwood Road, section 49. The loop passes a number of glacial ponds and begins opposite Campsite #23 on the shores of Fish Creek Pond, immediately beyond the campground gate. A gated park road forks to the right—you take it for approximately 50 yards and follow the red snowmobile markers as they lead to the right.

Quite near the beginning, you pass tiny Echo Pond, with its large sentinel white pines. The trail then proceeds over an esker with large yellow birch and hemlock crowning its top. In early May, the white blossoms of hobblebush and the yellow of trout lilies sparkle in the sunshine. Trout lily literally carpets the ground, though not all of the speckled leafed plants bloom.

At 0.8 mile there is a trail intersection, the way left is the 0.2-mile canoe carry to Fish Creek, right is the 200-foot carry to Follensby Clear Pond. Fish Creek has a boardwalk that takes you out into a strip of quaking bog bordering the creek. Tamarack and even some stunted white pine (on elevated portions) spring from the bog mat. In spring the small bell-like blossoms of leatherleaf are very noticeable.

The next pond you encounter, at 1.2 miles, after a pleasant walk of approximately half an hour through a handsome forest, is the aptly named Horseshoe Pond. A informal path shortcuts across the ends of the horseshoe then rejoins the trail and bends to follow the western shoreline. The marked trail follows the inside of the horseshoe circling around with almost continuous views of the pond.

As it winds along the western shoreline, the trail in a number of places is less than 200 yards from the shoreline, but the greenish coloring of this enticing pond is often blocked from view by conifers year round and even more by leaves of deciduous trees in summer. A short detour to the water or proper attention to the route so you do not detour away from the inside of the horseshoe reveals a shoreline of medium sized conifers. The trail continues through a small spruce swamp that can be very wet in early spring.

The trail crosses the outlet of Little Polliwog Pond on a bridge, then reaches, and for a very short distance follows, the carry trail between Horseshoe and Little Polliwog ponds. You turn right from this carry and angle north and at 2 miles reach a second canoe carry intersection. To the left, 75 yards away, lies Little Polliwog Pond, a tiny, conifer-clad pond. The carry to the right leads to Polliwog Pond, a sprawling glacial lake that attracts fishermen during spring and early summer for its landlocked salmon.

Beyond the intersection, you have a leisurely fifteen minute walk through a mature hemlock forest carpeted beneath by oxalis or wood sorrel. You can chew on its leaves; they provide a sharp, pungently pleasing taste. This is the plant known as shamrock in Ireland, and during the last century's great famine this attractive herb was used as emergency food rations by the starving populace.

At 2.7 miles you intersect a third canoe carry. To the right, the 0.1-mile yellow trail leads to a large, hidden bay on Polliwog Pond. The yellow markers to the left lead 0.2 mile to an intersection. If you detour straight ahead here you reach Middle Pond in 0.1 mile. It is long and narrow with large white pine along the shore. For the loop walk, go right, north, 0.1 mile to Floodwood Road and head west along it.

Floodwood Road here parallels Middle Pond. Follow it west for 1 mile to a marked left, south, turn and the start of the second leg of the snowmobile trail loop. You have come about 4 miles to this point, and have 3.7 miles to go.

The trail now takes a southerly direction, ascending a low ridge. Middle Pond is in sight to the east. A rustic bridge crosses the outlet to Middle Pond at 4.1 miles. One of the joys of the trail is the attractive stand of hemlock and yellow birch with the ever changing floral pattern under these woodland monarchs—red trillium and trout lilies in early spring, then painted trillium, and on to a late spring bouquet of pink moccasin flowers and bunchberry.

At 4.6 miles there is a fourth trail intersection with another of the region's numerous canoe carries. The yellow canoe carry to the left leads 0.25 mile to water lily-covered Middle Pond. You go right following the red-marked snowmobile trail, which after 0.1 mile turns sharply left, just before the carry trail turns off to lead downslope to a secluded bay of Floodwood Pond.

The trail now continues on a ridge crossing an inlet of Floodwood Pond on corduroy with views of the pond ever present on the right. At 5.4 miles, the connecting spur to the Otter Hollow Loop, section 46, heads right over a bridge spanning the outlet of Floodwood Pond. You continue along this lovely outlet until it reaches the eastern end of Little Square Pond. You walk along with Little Square Pond on your right until the pond narrows into an outlet creek, which is now called Fish Creek. The trail parallels that creek for a long but handsome stretch. Finally at 7.6 miles, the trail joins the park road, and a short jog left takes you to the beginning opposite campsite #23, for a total of 7.7 miles of trail. However, if you follow all the detours mentioned as carries to other ponds you add another mile or so, and four hours will not be enough.

46 Otter Hollow Loop

Snowmobile trail, cross-country skiing, fishing, hiking
8.1 miles, 4 hours, rolling terrain, maps VII and IX

Otter Hollow Loop is another of the trails that begin directly from the campgrounds, actually making a connection between both of them, and passing many of the region's entrancing bodies of water along the way. Although marked as a snowmobile trail, portions of the loop are used as canoe carries between the various bodies of water, and the whole loop provides a pleasant ramble.

The trail begins opposite campsite #104, which is approximately 0.5 mile from the campground entrance on NY 30. The trail leaves from the banks of Square Pond and proceeds northwest through a medium-sized white pine and white birch stand. Scattered red pine mark the gently rolling terrain. At 0.4 mile, the trail veers to the right, looping west to the shore of Copperas Pond under a canopy of mature hemlock.

The trail jogs back west to reach the northwest corner of Whey Pond at 0.8 mile. Long and somewhat narrow, framed by a shoreline of conifers and white birch, Whey Pond is managed as a special trout water fishery by DEC. There are restrictions to the number and size of both brook and rainbow trout that may be taken as well as restrictions on the type of bait used.

At approximately 1 mile, the trail begins to rise moderately and you notice more hardwoods in the canopy where mounds of glacial till provide better drained soils. As the trail begins a descent and becomes semi-wet in places, yellow birch and hemlock are again the dominant climax trees in the canopy.

Little Square Pond lies several hundred feet to the right of the trail at 1.3 miles. A small wooden bridge spans a small stream that drains into the pond. Because no trail leads to its shore, you have to leave the trail to explore the pond, which is conifer bordered, rimmed by ridges, and quiet, except during the summer when motorboats ply its waters.

Another stand of magnificent yellow birch and hemlock line the way as the trail passes over several medium steep ridges as it circles north then northeast around Little Square Pond. Part way along the north shore of Little Square Pond, the trail passes a lovely camp site on a rock promontory shaded by tall pines. Then the trail heads northwest over a rise and descends, at 2.8 miles, to a DEC sign stating "Floodwood Passage." A wooden bridge spans the passage here and leads to the Floodwood Loop

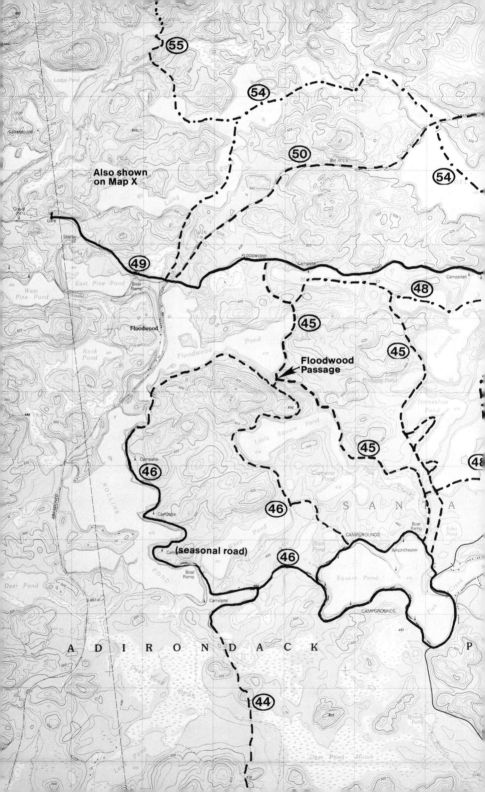

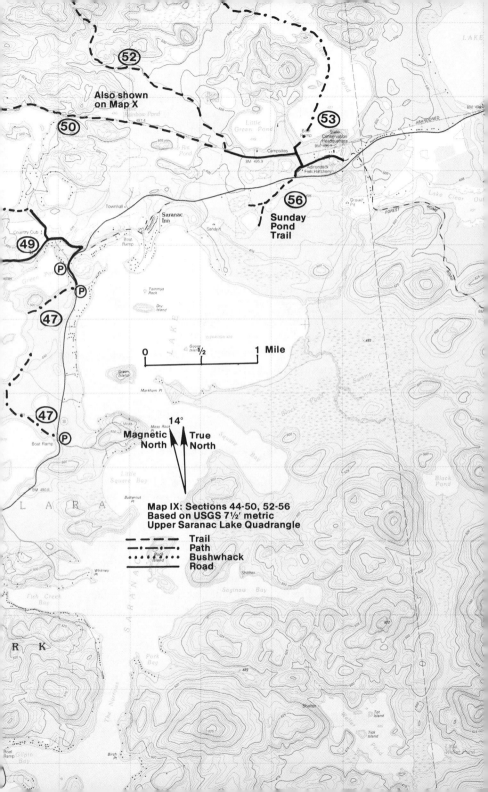

Also shown
on Map X

Sunday
Pond
Trail

0   ½   1 Mile

14°
Magnetic   True
North   North

Map IX: Sections 44-50, 52-56
Based on USGS 7½' metric
Upper Saranac Lake Quadrangle

— — — — Trail
— · — · — Path
· · · · · · · Bushwhack
———— Road

Trail, section 45, on the other side. If you wish to make an abbreviated loop here, you can take this trail back along the shore of Fish Creek until you reach the camp road. Following it west for 0.1 mile takes you back to the start of the Otter Hollow Loop where your car is parked. This shorter loop is approximately 5.5 miles in all.

Beyond the crossover at Floodwood Passage, your longer trail passes through a pole-sized stand of poplar and white birch, which attest to a fire from the early part of this century. Floodwood Pond, one of the large ponds on the loop, is in sight on the right for the next twenty minutes or so before the trail veers slightly away from the pond to finally reach Rollins Pond Campground at 4.2 miles, at a point where campsite #256 is located.

From this point, Floodwood Mountain seems to loom above Rollins Pond, and it would seem an inviting bushwhack, but it is posted, private land and so is off limits. From here a paved park road proceeds along the shore of Rollins Pond to arrive back at the starting point on the shores of Square Pond, after a total hike of 8.1 miles. Although it is paved, you can find solitude here in the off-season, and the view of Rollins Pond from along the road is worth the hike. Towering white pine and graceful white birch are encountered first, giving way after fifteen minutes or so to an extensive stand of hemlock. Porcupines may be seen in these hemlock during the winter. Branches cut by porcupine blanket the snow-covered surface and provide winter forage for the hard-pressed white-tailed deer.

Your route is generally south, winding along the shoreline of Rollins Pond. The road turns east, and just before it reaches Square Pond there is a red pine plantation. You will notice one difference right away between the native red pine and the exotic plantation. The denseness of the latter generally precludes any vegetation taking hold beneath the canopy, while light and vegetation increase under the more randomly-clumped native red pine. Even here the growth is generally various heath plants, particularly sheep laurel, because of the extreme acidity of the soil.

The route continues, passing the start of the Rollins Pond Trail to Lead Pond on the right at 7.1 miles. At 7.7 miles, at the shore of Square Pond, turn north, left, to arrive back at the beginning of the loop in the Fish Creek Campground.

47   Follensby Clear and Green Ponds Paths

Old tote roads, bushwhacks, canoeing, fishing, camping, old tent sites, exploring, map IX

Follensby Clear Pond, a large island-studded lake with handsome conifers and attractive campsites on its shores, runs in a general north-south axis parallel to nearby NY 30. The pond can be sampled by foot through an interconnected network of unmarked paths that link Follensby, Green Pond, and nearby NY 30 in a somewhat confusing maze.

One of these paths, which provides canoe access to Green Pond, begins on NY 30, approximately 0.3 mile south of the turnoff to Floodwood Pond. Park carefully on the side of the road here and proceed down the path 100 yards to the edge of Green Pond where another path comes in on the left. Take this past several other intersections, making a right turn at each, and in fifteen minutes of easy walking you arrive at a secluded bay of Follensby Clear Pond at a point where several attractive tent sites are located under a canopy of tall white pine.

One of the large wooded islands of Follensby beckons just a short distance away. The overwhelming impression you have is of blue and green, the mix of water and majestic evergreens, with a scattering of yellow birch. All this is more truly bucolic than wilderness— NY 30 is only 0.5 mile away and though the unmarked paths are usually empty, the brilliantly colored waters of the area are usually covered with boats all summer long.

Approximately 1.4 miles south of the Green Pond entranceway a short boat ramp leads west of NY 30, and cars may be parked at the DEC lot here for exploring the eastern shores of Follensby Clear Pond.

A somewhat indistinct path with unofficial sporadic red markings closely parallels the shore for approximately 1 mile. Primitive campsites, most with fire rings, are a frequent site along the shores. Many of these sites are remnants of old DEC approved tent sites, which were formerly very prevalent in this area. Although these tent sites had a long history here, many environmentalists and others argued that in addition to creating problems of overuse, they amounted to a private use of public land without legal authority. They were declared illegal under the State Land Master Plan and gradually removed.

An occasional majestic white pine still emerges above a hemlock on the shoreline. In late May and early June, the pink lady slipper is underfoot. After a while the path becomes quite difficult to follow, and you will have to bushwhack approximately 0.4 mile (keeping Follensby Clear Pond continuously in sight on the left) in order to reach the network of paths coming in from Green Pond on the north. The path you have been traveling can be followed for about 1 mile before you have to turn back or resort to the bushwhack on to the northern trails that come into Follensby Clear Pond from Green Pond and NY 30.

48   Fish Creek Pond Loop

Cross-country skiing
Approximately 9 miles, 5 hours, relatively level, map IX

One of the joys of the region's vast mixed surface of forest and water is the existence of a number of cross-country ski loops that use the frozen lakes and ponds and their interconnecting links, most often the carry trails. This increasingly popular pastime is locally known as "skiing the carries." Actually the number of these loops that may be made is limited in many respects only by the skier's imagination and proficiency in the use of a USGS topo map. The ponds are usually frozen enough to glide over by early January, and the marked carries are usually short and frequently ascend a conifer clad esker to drop down to the next body of water.

One of the most prominent of these loops is the circuit that begins and ends at Follensby Clear Pond. The ponds are all in the Saranac Lake Wild Forest, which surrounds Fish Creek Campground, but although snowmobiling is legal here, you will find that it is generally very light and should not interfere with skiing.

The circuit starts from the parking lot on NY 30 at a point where the outlet of Follensby Clear Pond flows into Fish Creek Pond. This is approximately 1.0 mile north of the campground entrance. You ski past several islands and narrows of Follensby Clear Pond for 2 miles to the northwest corner of the lake where the carry trail to Polliwog leads to that pond in 0.1 mile.

Ski west for 1 mile over Polliwog through its narrows to the far shore of its large hidden bay where the canoe carry trail, 0.4 mile long, takes off for Middle Pond. Glide about 0.5 mile across Middle Pond to its mid-southern shore to pick up the carry to Floodwood Pond, which you ski along for 0.4 mile to its eastern bay.

From here, a point 4.4 miles from the beginning, the route is south along the end of the Floodwood Loop described in section 45. Follow it for 3.6 miles as it parallels Fish Creek to the carry to Follensby Clear Pond, a left turn. Ski 0.2 mile along this carry, then cross Follensby Clear Pond in an east, then southeast direction for 0.7 mile to the boat ramp that was your beginning point.

The snow-clad stillness that only this winter wonderland can impart suffuses every glide of the nearly 9-mile trek.

St. Regis Canoe Area

ST. REGIS IS the premier canoeing area in the Adirondacks, and it is unique in the Park because it is the only designated Canoe Area. It consists of over 18,000 acres with 58 gorgeous lakes and ponds connected generally by rather short carries, trails for portages that link the ponds.

All the bodies of water are fringed with magnificent stands of mature red spruce, hemlock, white pine, and white birch. Equally impressive yellow birches become mixed with conifers a short way back from the shoreline. On the ridges and eskers thrust up between the ponds, noble specimens of sugar maple and beech appear, as they thrive on the better drained soils. These ponds are mainly in the watershed of the St. Regis but a few of them form the drainage of the very head of the Saranac basin. Some of the fish that inhabit these waters are brook and lake trout and landlocked salmon. These cold water species attest to the deep, cool ponds that were formed either by glacial scouring during the last ice age or by some action of its subsequent receding more than 10,000 years ago.

The area is managed as a Wilderness Area with motorized vehicles generally banned. (Certain exceptions are made for fish management activities.) The St. Regis Canoe Area has become so popular that there is talk of establishing at least one, and perhaps two, more canoe areas in the park when future additions to the Forest Preserve make this possible.

In winter it can be the most delightful place for cross-country skiing. It is difficult to predict when the ponds are safely frozen, but by January 1, it is possible to try the ice. The presence of ice fishing shanties on Lake Colby in Saranac Lake is usually a good indication that the area lakes and ponds are safe for travel. But as the French Canadian trapper said, " when you fall through the ice on snowshoes (or skis), your troubles, they are just starting."

If you canoe the St. Regis area in early June, with hordes of black flies and mosquitos deviling under your upturned canoe, you might feel you had discovered the area for the first time, or were certainly the first visitor of the year. But, in truth, the Canoe Area is remarkably popular most of the year.

Floodwood Road, see section 49, gives access to much of the St. Regis Canoe Area. A second access is from Fish Hatcher Road, a left turn 11.3 miles north of Wawbeek Corners on NY 30, about 2 miles north of

Map X: Sections 49-57
Based on USGS 7½′ metric
Upper Saranac Lake and
St. Regis Mtn. Quadrangles

——— Trail
—·—·— Path
····· Bushwhack
——— Road

0   ½   1 Mile

14°
Magnetic   True
North   North

Floodwood Road. Almost immediately you should see a DEC trailhead sign on the left. Cross the railroad tracks, making a sharp left at the sign pointing to Fish Pond, to follow the dirt road here for approximately 1 mile, as it parallels the Mohawk-Malone tracks. A small parking area is off a short spur to the right. You will pass a number of campsites on Little Green Pond on the way to this point. Trips 52 and 54 begin from the trailhead register placed at the end of the road, though as ski trips, they must begin back on Fish Hatchery Road, for the campground road is not plowed in winter.

49   Floodwood Road and Floodwood Mountain

Camping, short hike
5.5 mile road, drivable and plowed in winter, short informal trail, maps IX and X

Floodwood Road gives access to much of the St. Regis Canoe Area. The road passes through the Forest Preserve for most of its first 5.5 miles and this stretch is plowed in winter. All along it are lovely campsites, some near the water, all quite accessible from the road. They are numbered and you can camp anywhere along the road for up to three days, without a permit, but you must camp only at these designated and numbered sites.

Floodwood Road is a west turn from NY 30, 9.2 miles north of the intersection of NY 3 and 30 at Wawbeek Corners. At 0.35 mile, Floodwood Road is a left fork. Just short of 1 mile the carry to Hoel Pond is on the north side of the road. At 3.2 miles there is a marked snowmobile trail to the south and at 4 miles you cross a one-lane bridge. At 4.25 miles the road crosses the Mohawk-Malone Railroad tracks, section 50, and nearby there is a parking area and turnaround. The canoe carry to Long Pond is at 5.25 miles. At 5.5 miles, the road reaches a newly-acquired parcel of state land, a 4,600-acre tract that was originally the Floodwood Boy Scout Reservation. This purchase opens up a short hike to the top of Floodwood Mountain, a charming and isolated peak, with glimpses of the wild, boreal region that unfurls from the base of the little mountain in all directions.

The path, marked as a private trail by the scouts, starts, 0.8 mile from the gate that used to mark the end of the road, 5.5 miles from NY 30. The new

St. Regis Pond

gate is just beyond this point, and at present there is no indication that the road will be plowed beyond the old gate.

Starting on the left side of the road, the path goes under a wooden arch and heads through a meadow which is slowly recovering from an old fire. At 0.4 mile, a wooden bridge takes you over a creek, and the old road that the path follows now heads through second growth hardwoods to a fork at 0.9 mile. Veering right at the fork brings you to the start of the 500-foot climb, which is marked by a two-foot round boulder, a relic of melting glacial ice. The path is fairly well worn and marked by red discs. It is level at first and heads south by southwest along a brook before beginning a fairly sharp ascent at 0.4 mile. Northern hardwoods, mostly beech, surround the path.

The summit is 0.8 mile from the fork. Rollins Pond lies immediately below and St. Regis Mountain lies several miles to the north. In the southwest, Mount Matumbla and Mount Arab loom over the mostly flat boreal forest that is so typical of the area.

50 Mohawk-Malone Railroad Ski Trail

Cross-country skiing
6.5 miles one way, 3½ hours, level, maps IX and X

An abandoned 6.5-mile stretch of the old Mohawk-Malone Railroad track lies idle between Little Green Pond and Floodwood Road. It goes through an attractive slice of north country terrain entirely in the Forest Preserve and makes a pleasant cross-country ski jaunt in the winter if you leave cars at both Floodwood Road and the trailhead sign for Fish Pond, which is located on Fish Hatchery Road. See the introduction to this chapter for trailhead directions. The railroad borders the Canoe Area, so snowmobiles are permitted, and you will have to watch for them, though their tracks do make a nice base for skiing.

Short trails lead from this main route to both Little Green Pond and Bone Pond. The latter is 0.4 mile from the eastern trailhead and follows the truck trail of section 50 over a rise and into a hollow where Bone Pond is tucked between ridges. This is a good preliminary for the main ski trail along the abandoned railroad tracks.

The route going west along the tracks starts amidst a conifer plantation, which, on its south side, extends to Little Green Pond. Rat Pond lies on your left at 1 mile. A promontory, jutting out into the midpoint of that pond is quite attractive and often visited by white-tailed deer, which browse under the white cedar on the far shore. The inlet to Rat Pond is dammed, flooding tamarack and spruce that extend upstream to the pond.

Skiing along the tracks, you look down on Rat Pond's north shore. From Rat Pond, it is approximately another mile to Little Rainbow Pond. The track splits the pond with the largest portion lying to the right of the tracks. The serenity of winter is an amazing contrast to the vibrant intensity of life in summer. An amble along the tracks to this spot in early June reveals numerous painted turtles, both basking on logs and up on the tracks laying eggs. Myriad dragonflies clutter the airwaves over the trail and water as they engage in their annual breeding cycle. Yellow water lilies brighten the water's surface. Uncounted green frogs give their mating call in a hollow banjo voice that increases to an agitated frenzy as females appear on the scene.

In winter, the silence and starkness of the snowy scene is pervasive. Another ten minutes of skiing 0.5 mile, and the railroad tracks reach the shore of Hoel Pond, just north of where the outlet of Little Rainbow Pond flows into Hoel. South of the tracks here there are a number of private camps along the shores of Hoel Pond, reached by private road.

After skiing about another twenty minutes, another mile, you arrive at 3.7 miles at a spot where the railroad embankment separates sprawling Hoel Pond from crookneck-shaped Turtle Pond. The waters of the St. Regis Canoe Area lie everywhere in sight—now locked in the glistening white embrace of winter. After skiing for another twenty-five minutes or so, at about 5.3 miles, you reach the place where a causeway carrying the tracks threads through a huge flooded swamp with countless dead trees stretching out on both sides of the embankment. Again, beaver are responsible for the flooding.

At a point 5.7 miles from Little Green Pond, you reach a charming five-acre body of water. A well-marked path leads 1.7 miles from it to Floodwood Road at a point opposite Floodwood Loop. Because of the amount of blowdown across the trail, it is not suitable as a cross-country ski route. Continue on the tracks, and just before you reach Floodwood Road, you see on your right a fish-barrier dam erected to protect upstream game fishing at both Fish Creek and Rollins Pond campgrounds. Floodwood Road is at 6.5 miles.

51   Chickadee Creek and Roiley Pond

Cross-country skiing, bushwhack, map X

Nearly everyone who has spent much time around Upper St. Regis Lake is familiar with Chickadee Creek, a wetlands museum-piece that flows its entire winding way through a swath of bog and marsh a thousand feet wide and a mile and a half long. This flat, open, soggy ground makes for difficult (not to mention wet) going during the warm months, but, in the winter, the valley of Chickadee Creek becomes an inviting but little-used highway for skiers and snowshoers.

This trip begins on private land. Please respect it to assure continued access. Start at the Upper St. Regis Post Office off NY 30 between Lake Clear Junction and Paul Smiths. You can head up beside (not on) the creek right from the south end of the lake, or you can follow the jeep trail that runs southwest from the post office and crosses the creek about 0.25 mile above its mouth. If the snow is not deep or solid enough to carry you over the bog's heath plants, or if it has not been cold enough to make good ice on the sloughs and spring-pools, there is another jeep trail that continues parallel to the creek almost to its source at Roiley Pond. This road is not shown on the St. Regis Mountain metric quadrangle, but it breaks from the main trail where the latter turns abruptly westward to go down out of the woods toward the creek. The spur trail stays in the forest, continuing a southwesterly course.

Roiley Pond is a modest and somewhat lonesome body of water surrounded by evergreens. If you are feeling adventurous, you can proceed from Roiley up along the outlet of Little Long Pond—an interesting bushwhack on skis.

Once at Little Long Pond, you can go just about anywhere.

Along Fish Pond Trail

52 Fish Pond Truck Trail

Cross-country skiing, hiking, fishing
4.6 miles one way, 2 miles round trip of side excursions, 4 to
6 hours, relatively level, maps IX and X

A pleasant 9.2-mile hike or ski trip heads along and returns on the path of an old DEC truck trail and several interconnecting canoe carries that intersect it. The truck trail is now closed to all motorized access. Its ultimate destination is Fish Pond, but it also gives access to three short carries. Three interior ponds, St. Regis, Grassy, and Ochre, are easily approached as side trips from the truck trail, and round trips to each adds a total of 2 miles to the round trip.

The sheer joy of the route is enough justification for making the trip. You pass magnificent stands of hardwoods interspersed with imposing spruce and white pines. Along the way you also encounter an imposing white cedar swamp. But, the ultimate reward for the trip is the seclusion of Fish Pond.

The trailhead is from Fish Hatchery Road (see this chapter's introduction). The gated roadway continues past the trail register, 1 mile from Fish Hatchery Road. You begin beneath a towering canopy of yellow birch, hemlock, and red spruce that changes to sugar maple and beech on the well-drained soils of the several moderately steep ridges, which the trail crosses. Just beyond Little Green Pond, the trail comes within 0.2 mile of Bone Pond, then turns west. Beyond it skirts the perimeter of extensive wetlands where the cover grades into white cedar and mammoth white pine.

The trail undulates rapidly as it ascends and descends the crest of several small hills along the way. You find this adds just a little bit of extra spice to a cross-country ski trip! The trail appears to receive more use by skiers than by hikers in summer.

After about 1 hour of walking, 2.5 miles of trail, a wide jeep trail comes in on the right. It leads 0.2 mile to a secluded bay of St. Regis Pond, which is a large glacial lake. A barrier dam for fish management has been constructed at its outlet. Sphagnum and heath plants in the open bog border the lake, which is further framed by encircling spruce and fir.

Return to the main trail and after a few minutes of easy walking, you will notice the canoe carry to Grassy Pond coming in on the left at 2.7 miles. This trail leads in 0.5 mile to the shores of Grassy Pond, so named because

Looking north down inlet of St. Regis Pond

of its encircling rim of sedges. Towering conifers rise behind its grassy border.

Again retracing your steps to the main trail, continue on it until the canoe carry to Ochre Pond comes in from the right at 3.6 miles. Like the others, this route has a small DEC sign, but in any event, the relatively wide tote road is quite obvious at the point it joins the main trail. It leads 0.3 mile down the tote road to a gem of water bordered by a forest of hemlock, yellow birch, and spruce that is so majestic that there is speculation that it might be an original, old-growth forest. No matter, Ochre Pond has a magnificent setting. Across its waters on the northwest shore lies the route of the Ridge Trail described as part of the St. Regis Pond Ski Loop, section 53.

Again returning to the main trail, continue northwest on it for another mile to Fish Pond. Along the way, you pass a ridge to the right of the trail. This ridge flanks wetlands that lie on the rim of the upper reaches of Mud Pond, a relatively large glacial pond surrounded by an arc of hills. The trail approaches Fish Pond at a narrow marshy bay, and there are several primitive campsites along the shore. Over the horizon many more of the small jewel-like bodies of water are strewn profusely throughout the canoe area. Right now, leave them for another day and return to the trailhead directly on the main trail, for a round trip of 11.2 miles if you have made all the side excursions described.

53 St. Regis Pond Cross-country Ski Loop

Cross-country skiing
10.3 miles, 5 hours, mostly level, maps IX and X

A truly breathtaking ski loop through a realm of majestic green conifers, glistening white snow, and ice clad ponds uses a chain of frozen ponds and carries. The loop follows the famous St. Regis Esker under a towering canopy of white pine, yellow birch, and hemlock. It finishes along the Fish Pond Truck Trail of section 52.

Little Clear Pond is the starting point of this loop. See chapter introduction for directions to Fish Hatchery Road and the jeep road to Little Clear Pond.

Ski down the main trail and a short distance, less than 100 yards, after crossing the Mohawk-Malone Railroad tracks, take the ramp on the right to the shore of Little Clear Pond. From here ski north, paralleling its west shore. Go into the large western bay about 1.8 miles from the start and notice the small DEC sign on the far side pointing out the canoe carry to St. Regis Pond. The carry ascends a ridge and then descends rather quickly to enter St. Regis Pond at a southeast bay, at 2.3 miles. Ski across St. Regis Pond for nearly 1.5 miles to the northwestern corner of the northwest bay. Here you find the next carry, the beginning of the Ridge Trail. On the way you pass several of St. Regis Pond's islands. St. Regis Mountain stands as a protective sentinel above the pond.

Another carry trail starts in the southwestern corner of the northwestern bay, near the outlet where the water of St. Regis Pond cascades over a small fish barrier dam to become the headwaters of the West Branch of the St. Regis River. This is the carry trail to the Fish Pond Truck Trail and can be used to make a shorter loop. Use it to reach the Truck Trail, then head southeast past its trailhead to the old Mohawk-Malone Railroad tracks and out to where your car is parked. This abbreviated loop is about 8 miles long, and ends exactly as the longer one described below.

For the longer loop to Fish Pond, you follow the Ridge Trail; and many of the best delights are yet to come. That trail starts at the northwestern end of the bay at a point above the old trail that follows the shoreline of the West Branch of the St. Regis. In a short while, about 0.5 mile, the Ridge Trail reaches Ochre Pond, a hidden jewel framed on all sides by old-growth forest. Cross to the west shore of the pond and at 4.5 miles begin an ascent of the striking St. Regis Esker. This famous esker is one of the largest in the park. The sandy soil underneath it, a remnant of an underground stream that once coursed beneath glacial ice, provides a perfect matrix so that the white pine, hemlock, and spruce that line the trail attain their maximum growth. The spot is even more impressive in winter than in summer.

Ski along the esker for 0.7 mile to a fork on the ridge. The right fork leads to Mud Pond. If you continue straight ahead, you reach Fish Pond at 5.7 miles at a point on a headland that juts out into the main body of the lake. Ski across the southeast bay to the Fish Pond Truck Trail landing. Ignore the blue markers on the ridge trail as they lead off to the left a short distance before you reach the lake. The old trail here made a crossing of the West Branch before arriving at the landing. The wooden bridge, however, has washed away and the route is not suitable for skiing.

Follow the Fish Pond Truck Trail, section 52, 4.6 miles back to the trailhead and then ski the railroad tracks back to your parked vehicle.

54   Long Pond-Hoel Pond Ski Tour
Cross-country skiing
6 miles, 3 to 4 hours, level, maps IX and X

Another route that lies mostly in the St. Regis Canoe Area lends itself to an ideal Nordic ski jaunt. It circles from Hoel Pond to Long Pond and back out to the Floodwood Road. Spot one car 4 miles west of NY 30 on Floodwood Road at the railroad tracks, where several parking spots are usually plowed out. The canoe carry trail is 30 feet beyond the railroad track.

To reach the beginning of the circuit at the boat ramp to Hoel Pond, take the first right fork from Floodwood Road and proceed along Golf Course Road to the edge of the woods. Cars will usually have to be carefully parked here as the next 250 yards leading to the boat ramp are not usually plowed. This is, however, a good place to begin the ski route.

Head northwest across Hoel Pond for about 1.2 miles until you reach the railroad tracks. You have to climb up and over the tracks (it is steep!) to continue on the other side. You are now skiing on Turtle Pond. If you want to add to this circuit, you can ski to Clamshell Pond, less than a 2-mile round trip from Turtle Pond along a carry route that begins just east of an inlet stream and leads north over a ridge before descending to Clamshell.

For the through circuit, ski northwest across Turtle Pond and along its outlet that leads into Slang Pond at 3.2 miles. It is about 0.5 mile across to the southwest corner of Slang Pond where a canoe carry leads 0.2 mile to Long Pond's eastern shore.

A second possible addition to this circuit leads to Nellie and Bessie Ponds along a canoe carry trail that begins at the northern lobe of Long Pond. This round-trip detour is more than 2 miles long, though relatively level. Yet another trip from a western bay of Long Pond leads to Mountain Pond, see section 55, about a 2.5-mile loop from the main circuit.

To complete the circuit ski loop, ski southwest, then south, two-thirds of the way (about 1.5 miles) down Long Pond until you see the canoe carry to Floodwood Pond on the southern shore. The carry is about 0.7 mile and you ski about fifteen minutes along it to reach Floodwood Road and the car you have spotted there. All the side excursions will more than double the distance, adding 7 miles to the 6-mile circuit.

55 Long Pond Mountain

Trail and bushwhack, canoeing, fishing
1.2-mile trail, 1.5-mile round-trip bushwhack, 850-foot vertical rise, maps IX and X

Nestled deep in the folds of the St. Regis Canoe Area, Long Pond Mountain can be scaled only after a 2-mile canoe paddle, a walk on a trail, and a bushwhack up its trailless slopes. It is certainly worth the effort; for not only do you have an exciting view of the whole canoe area, from the top you will feel as if all the earth is in harmony.

All was not harmony on the mountain in the past, however. A series of violent events has conspired to leave the mountain top generally free of trees. The first event was the "great windfall" of 1845, a tornado or series of tornados that swept northeast. A chain of Windfall Ponds and streams points almost to Long Pond Mountain, so it has been theorized that those storms devastated the mountain also. Fires, early in this century, swept the mountain, burning the duff and vegetable soils to bedrock. A natural fire, this one caused by lightning, burned several acres on the summit in 1966.

To reach this uplifting bushwhack, drive 4 miles west on Floodwood Road to the Mohawk-Malone Railroad tracks. Continue 1 mile more to a jeep road that leads off to the right a short distance to a parking area for Long Pond. Your trip begins here with a paddle to the canoe carry to Mountain Pond.

Cross Long Pond in an easterly direction until the lake begins to veer north. Watch for a large bay that opens to the west. The beginning of the ascent is on the northern side of the bay and is marked with a small wooden sign as the canoe carry to Mountain Pond.

From this point, it is 0.6 mile to the shores of Mountain Pond. The trail passes through a plantation of exotic Norway spruce, a curious anomaly in an area managed as natural wilderness. In summer, purplish-blue masses of pickerel weed fill the shallows. Look for signs that white-tailed deer have been browsing its leaves and spikes.

At Mountain Pond, you will see a fisherman's path circling the pond to the right, east. Follow it around to the far side of the pond and then just as it starts to circle back on the west side, set your compass for a due north reading and begin climbing.

The climb gradually becomes steeper. Keep as close as possible to a due north reading as several steep rockface ledges impede the way to the west of north. Your route is mainly through a second growth, which is reclaiming the forest. In several areas, bedrock outcrops attest to the ferocity of the fires. These are delightful places to take a short break.

You continue up, skirting several hollows that dip steeply between ridges and crossing one false summit. Finally you reach the flat, grassy summit. Below you the circuit from Hoel Pond to Long Pond is clearly etched in the green landscape. The stack and tower of the village of Tupper Lake lie to the southwest, while to the southeast on a clear day you can pick out the distant High Peaks. To the northeast you see the fire tower on St. Regis Mountain. That mountain frames Fish Pond, which lies to the southwest of it, while St. Regis Pond is cozily snuggled at the foot of the mountain's southeast side.

Fish Pond lies to the southwest. To the northwest are the extensive private lands of the Rockefeller and Ross estates and beyond them lie the even more extensive forests, bogs, and mountains owned by Champion Paper Company. All these views on a bushwhack climb that takes less than an hour!

56 Sunday Pond

Nature walk, cross-country skiing, marked snowmobile and horse trail
1 mile, ¹/₂ hour, level, maps IX and X

Sunday Pond is a minute example of a true kettle—a depression created by a chunk of glacial ice that persisted for a time after the glacier retreated.

Boreal forest surrounds the boggy shores of the kettle that is depressed below the level of the surrounding land so the pond has no outlet. The only water entering the pond is precipitation or the slight drainage from its surroundings. The resulting acidic environment inspires a nature walk to discover the limited array of plants that survive here.

A very short, stimulating walk leads to this pond and a second even tinier one from NY 30. The marked trailhead is 2.1 miles east of Floodwood Road. It begins along an old tote road that heads south between two houses, approximately 50 yards before the intersection of Fish Hatchery Road, which is on the north.

The trail reaches Forest Preserve after 30 yards and continues wide and level, passing through second growth forest. A gradual descent follows, and you can see Sunday Pond through the trees at 0.6 mile. The trail then encircles the pond to come to a landing at 1 mile. Here the tote road turns right and shortly after leaves the Forest Preserve to enter posted, private property.

In winter, ski out on the pond to enjoy the pines, hemlocks, and spruce that surround the circular pond. Later on, goldeneye ducks and hooded mergansers will take over the surface of the pond. Retracing your steps for about 0.1 mile and turning left for 0.3 mile, you can sample an enchanting heath bog mat with an even tinier pond at its center. This route is best experienced in spring and summer when pitcher plants grow profusely over the bog mat. Wood ducks call from nearby perches. The trail straight leads also to private houses on NY 30, so retrace your steps to return to the trailhead. The total walking distance described is about 2.6 miles.

57 St. Regis Mountain

Lean-to, manned fire tower, hiking, snowshoeing
5 miles round trip, 3 hours, 1250-foot vertical rise, maps X and XI

Looming over the northern section of the St. Regis Canoe Area and visible from many of the ponds in the area stands the impressive presence of its namesake mountain, crowned with a manned fire tower. Climbing it gives you a glimpse into the working of the fire towers that are now generally considered obsolete for fire detection except in special instances such as this one. The hiker who reaches the summit is also rewarded with the magnificent panorama of forested, rolling hills and sparkling waters that unfurls below and fades into the distant blue of the higher mountains in the High Peaks region.

Take Keese Mills Road west from its junction with NY 30 at Paul Smith's. Turn left at 2.4 miles on a gravel road and follow it until further progress is blocked by the gates of a large private estate—Camp Topridge. Trailhead parking is on the right. Camp Topridge, once owned by Marjorie Post, the socialite of breakfast cereal fame, was bequeathed to New York State. In an action deemed controversial by some, the state resold the buildings to Roger Jakubowski and transferred the bulk of the land around the buildings to the Forest Preserve. What may be even more controversial is the rumor that Jakubowski will attempt to buy a tract to the north of his land over which are located the access road and the beginning of the St. Regis Mountain Trail. If that occurs, forcing the closing of the trail, the state could build a trail from the north, along the route that this section suggests as a possible bushwhack descent from the mountain.

The hike begins by following the marked trail as it winds through mostly hardwood forest over private lands at first. After approximately thirty minutes of hiking, about 1 mile, you pass some outbuildings of the estate, then cross a dirt road that is used by the fire tower observer to reach his cabin. You pass that cabin at 1.5 miles; a pleasantly situated DEC lean-to is to the right of the cabin.

Both painted and wake robin trilliums brighten the forest floor here in late spring. The trail becomes gradually steeper and the trees shorter. White birch attest to fires that swept this peak. Just before you emerge from the trees there is a path to the left to a bare rock outcrop with views. The summit is generally bald. You reach it at 2.5 miles. Pin cherry, dwarf conifers, and carpets of blueberries flourish between open rock patches. Climb the fire tower if the observer is on duty and gaze down on the endless panorama of green and blue beneath the mountain.

The summit became bald in August of 1876 when Verplanck Colvin established a triangulation tower on its summit. He wrote:

"The view was impeded by brush and dead trees, and one of the guides suggested that they be collected in heaps and burned. This was accordingly commenced, but to our confusion and alarm in a very few moments the fire proved the master, and spreading with a fearful roar, sweeping up into the dead tree tops, caused us to beat a most hasty and ignominious retreat, barely escaping with our instruments down the ledges before the torrent of flame swept across the summit and wrapped it all in fierce conflagration. As night came on, the scene became one of wild sublimity. From our camp, where we

Looking across St. Regis Pond toward St. Regis Mountain

watched with anxiety, we looked up out of the darkness at the sea of flame. Now it reached the brink of the cliff above, and soon the tall trees became columns of live coals, till burned away at the base they would bend, totter and fall down the cliff like bars of white hot iron, carrying the flames down into fresh ground, where the peat-like soil—dry as tinder—instantly caught the blaze and spread the conflagration. . . . All night the fire raged; the air was thick with smoke, and the mountain had, indeed, the appearance of a volcano in violent eruption—lighting the country around. Suddenly sharp but deep reverberations sounded above the crackling and roaring of the fire, and told of the explosions of the rock, deprived of its water of crystallization by the fervent heat."

The adventurous might want to try an alternate descent from the mountain. A fairly direct bushwhack route takes you to Keese Mills Road a little to the west of the bridge over the St. Regis River and just over 2 miles west of the road to the tower.

Head west along the open rock of the summit, descending a bit. A nose of the mountain descends more gradually headed toward magnetic north. Head down along it, staying to the west of the nose and to the east of a draw that heads in the same direction. A stream quickly forms in that draw. On your heading you will descend fairly rapidly. The forest is open old-growth hardwoods at first, then you pass through a layer of hemlock stands. You descend 900 feet in just over a mile, then your route along the heading toward magnetic north becomes more gradual. On the lower slopes you will find a stand of black cherry. You may intersect one of many logging roads that weave across the lower slopes as you traverse relatively level ground on your final approach to the road. The last nearly half mile is gentle to almost level through abandoned fields with young pine trees, open and easy terrain for a bushwhack.

The 2-mile descent should take no more than two hours. The forest cover is quite lovely. This is a favorite route for those who like to climb St. Regis in the winter on snowshoes. It would also make a good route for a new trail should the state fail to acquire the lower slopes of the mountain over which the trail now passes.

Paul Smiths

APOLLOS (PAUL) SMITH visited the north country to hunt and fish several times before he decided in 1852 to build a hotel and move there permanently. His first hotel, Hunter's Home, for men only, was built about a mile from Loon Lake near the North Branch of the Saranac River. It was an instant success, and he followed it with several shrewd land purchases. A wealthy patron encouraged him to buy land on Lower St. Regis Pond and construct a much larger hotel there. This was finished in 1859 and was also a great success, some said due to his wife's good cooking and his story telling.

Not only was he a clever raconteur, but he continued to purchase land, acquiring upwards of forty thousand acres of which five thousand were along the Saranac River. He owned ten lakes and many miles of streams. He logged his own land, built a sawmill to mill it, and founded Paul Smith's Electric Light and Power and Railroad Company. The company had power plants at Union Falls and Franklin Falls on the Saranac. The electric railroad, completed in 1906 to serve the hotel, connected with the New York Central Adirondack Division and replaced his stagecoach line, which had brought guests from the Delaware and Hudson's Chateaugay Line at Bloomingdale.

Much of his land and fortune were left to build the college that bears his name. It is spelled Paul Smith's, while the hamlet with his name has no apostrophe. To this day, the college specializes in the two things he held most important, forestry and hotel management.

The college is near the intersection of NY 30 and 192. You can reach it by driving north from Wawbeek Corners on the winding road past the St. Regis Canoe Area and Lake Clear. You can also reach the intersection by driving north from Saranac along Broadway, through Donnelly's corners with a magnificent view of the Bloomingdale Bog with Whiteface Mountain beyond, through Gabriels and west on Easy Street, which is NY 192.

58 The Red Dot Trail

Hiking, nature trail, cross-country skiing
2.5 miles, 1 hour, level, map XI

An excellent self-guided, interpretive trail leads through terrain shaped by glacial outwash, across eskers, and beside glacial ponds. Along the way, aspects of local flora and fauna are pointed out. The Red Dot Trail is a loop with several side trails, including three yellow access spurs. One of these begins from the parking lot of St. Gabriel's Church, which is diagonally across from the college at the intersection of NY 30 and 192.

Beyond the registration booth, the trail takes you generally northeast, then east. In ten minutes you cross an old road and shortly beyond you reach an intersection. The way right leads to the shore of Church Pond East. Nearby are the Cathedral Pines, towering remnants of a virgin forest, which reach well over one hundred feet.

Captions are set along the main trail. One refers to the Adirondack mouse, which has just recently recolonized in the park and has been sighted nearby.

The trail reaches a "T," where you can walk either way to make the Red Trail Loop. If you go right, you shortly pass the Church Pond Lean-to and beyond it a footbridge over a canal connecting Church and Little Osgood ponds. Across the bridge, a second yellow spur heads south, leading to the cemetery and NY 192. You go straight to yet another intersection (all these distances are very short). A third yellow spur heads east to a dirt road, which again is an access from NY 192.

You turn north across a second footbridge, this one over a channel that is part of the early century canal system dug to eliminate the carries between Osgood Pond and the churches at Paul Smiths. Because fishing for smallmouth bass and brook trout is excellent here, the ponds and connecting canals get fairly heavy use by both fishermen and canoers.

Beyond the bridge, the Red Trail forks; the way right loops toward the shore of Osgood Pond, the way left passes a lean-to at Little Osgood Pond. The two trails rejoin at the shore of Osgood Pond. The rejoined Red Dot Trail continues west along the shore beside log bench resting places to a lean-to. Here the Red Dot Trail heads south to complete the circle near the shore of Church Pond; while the shore route continues west beside Osgood Pond. The shores of Osgood Pond are a mixture of Forest Preserve and private land with a number of rustically elegant camps, most dating to the era when Paul Smith's Hotel was the region's main attraction.

The lean-tos are owned by Paul Smith's College, but may be used by the public.

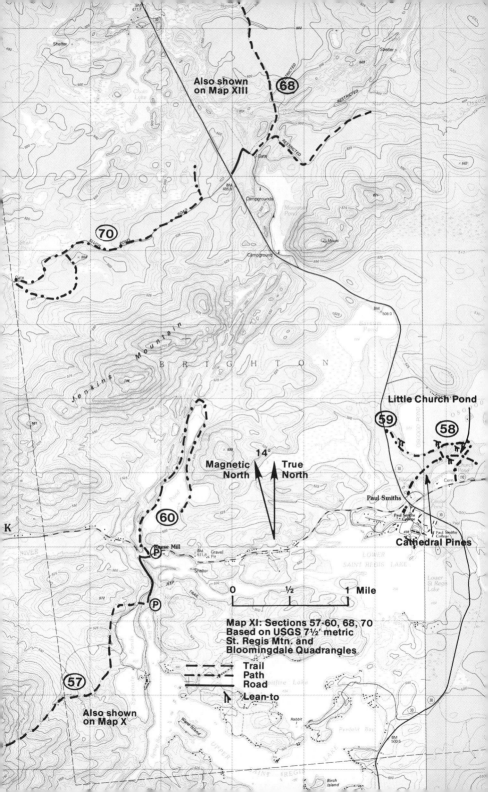

Also shown
on Map XIII

68

70

Also shown
on Map X

57

Little Church Pond

59

58

Magnetic
North

14°

True
North

60

Paul Smiths

Cheese Mill

Cathedral Pines

P

P

0   ½   1 Mile

Map XI: Sections 57-60, 68, 70
Based on USGS 7½' metric
St. Regis Mtn. and
Bloomingdale Quadrangles

Trail
Path
Road

Lean-to

Along the Red Dot Trail

59 The Adirondack Visitors Interpretive Center

Map XI

At long last, close to a century after its founding in 1892, the Adirondack Park is to receive the element of recognition common to most other American parks. The Adirondacks will have two Visitors Interpretive Centers (VIC), a main one at Paul Smith's College and a smaller center at Newcomb. These centers will be analogous in many respects to those at such national parks as Yellowstone or Great Smoky, but there will be distinct differences as they will represent the fact that this park comprises both public and private lands. Run and staffed by the Adirondack Park Agency, the centers are tentatively scheduled to open sometime in 1989.

It would seem to be a most difficult task to depict all the varied splendors of the Adirondack Park in one or even two centers. Yet a recent visit to the main center at Paul Smith's revealed that as difficult as it seems this will be accomplished. There, the main building, constructed in the style of the Adirondack Great Camp, will be situated on a bluff overlooking a broad marsh. It will have a theater to show films on the park, displays, and tourist information. Exhibits will depict the human and natural history of the park, wildlife, ecological processes, and forestry management.

On the 2800-acre tract leased from the college are represented all the Adirondack ecosystems except the sub-alpine spruce-fir and the alpine tundra that are restricted to the High Peaks. Particularly well represented are open peat land, tamarack-black spruce bog, red spruce-balsam fir swamp, open marsh, lakeshore, and beaver pond and meadows. The first two especially, and possible the third, are under-represented in the Forest Preserve at present because they are restricted to this wild region of currently almost exclusively private forest land.

Six interpretive trails will wind through all the representative ecosystems. The trails will be suitable for both hiking and cross-country skiing, while at the same time being informative. When finished, they will present a network of interconnecting loops. Their base will be a matrix of bark chips of hardwood trees that remain less slippery when wet (the universal Adirondack condition) than traditional softwoods.

A well-designed trail for the handicapped, constructed mainly of gravel paths and wooden boardwalks, is a first for the Adirondacks. All trails will have viewing platforms in especially scenic or instructive areas. All trails will feature highlights of Adirondack flora and fauna, in addition to natural habitats and forest management techniques.

The following is a brief synopsis of the six projected interpretive trails at the Adirondack VIC at the Paul Smith's site. Most will start in the vicinity of the parking area adjacent to the main center building. Drive 0.8 mile north of Paul Smith's College on NY 30 and turn west for a short distance on a gravel road to the parking area. The following is a brief description of each of the trails.

A - *Barnum Rock Interpretive Trail* has easy access for the physically handicapped. Wayside exhibits, elevated viewing platforms, and resting benches are featured along its 3600-foot length.

B - *Heron Marsh Interpretive Trail* is also 3600 feet long with wayside exhibits, resting benches, and viewing platforms, some of which overlook the lovely marsh.

C - *Forest Ecology Trail* is 7400 feet in length, of which approximately 400 feet follows the existing Blue Dot Trail. One highlight of the trail is a 250-foot floating bridge.

D - *Shingle Mill Falls Interpretive Trail* follows the remaining 3600 feet of the Blue Dot Trail and has a restroom facility.

Along the Red Dot Trail

E - *Silvacultural Interpretive Trail*, 5600 feet long, has, in addition to the wayside exhibit, observation platforms, and resting benches, a Sugar Maple Exhibit that explains current forestry techniques practiced in the Adirondacks.

F - *Barnum Pond Interpretive Trail* is the longest, over 7400 feet, with an extended boardwalk along the fragile shores of the pond.

60 Long and Black Ponds

Hiking, canoeing, camping, fishing, cross-country skiing
1.5 miles, 1 hour, relatively level, map XI

A part of the longest esker in the region borders the west side of Long and Black ponds at the base of Jenkins Mountain. The land here belongs to Paul Smith's College, which kept the westside trail open to the public. It is part of the land leased to the state for the Visitors Interpretive Center (VIC) and it is anticipated that the west side trail and access to the lake will remain open to the public. There are currently five lean-tos on the two ponds. They were built by forestry management students and are currently open to the public, but their future use may change because of the proximity of the ponds to the VIC.

Drive west from Paul Smiths for 2.5 miles to Keese Mills. The St. Regis Presbyterian Church is on the south side of the road and opposite it to the north, just across a stream, is a parking area that can accommodate eight to ten cars. It is only 100 feet from the parking area to a dock where you can launch your canoe. By canoe, you can explore the eastern lobe of Black Pond, paddle to a landing at the northwest end of the pond, use the access trail to portage your canoe the 0.3 mile to Long Pond, and fish its waters, which are noted for an abundance of relatively small trout.

The access trail (which might better be called a path, since it has no formal markings) starts in the parking area and takes you along the west bank of the outlet for 0.2 mile to Black Pond. The first lean-to is at the southwest corner of the pond. You walk along the shore north beneath the esker to the landing dock at 0.8 mile. The trail continues north, no more than 20 feet from the outlet of Long Pond, then follows the west shore of Long Pond north beneath the steep slopes of the esker to a lean-to that is near the northern end of the pond.

The other three lean-tos are all on the east shores. They are reached by a canoe paddle, or the segment of trail on the east shore. About halfway between the ponds, a path forks east across the stream connecting the ponds. A short path leads north from the crossing to the lean-to on the east shore of Long Pond. The path south leads over a bridge over the channel that separates the main body of Black Pond from its eastern lobe. One lean-to is to the south of the channel, overlooking it, the second is on the next promontory to the south.

There is a short path, about 0.2 mile, from the north end of Long Pond, still along the base of the esker, to Jenkins Mountain Road, a logging road.

Along the Red Dot Trail

This point can be the jump off for an exciting bushwhack northwest over the esker, past kettle ponds, and up the draw between the summits of Jenkins Mountain. The southeastern faces of both summits are ringed with steep slopes and cliffs. There are great views and interesting flora. This bushwhack may not be accessible to the public in the future, so check either at Paul Smith's or at the VIC.

Jenkins Mountain was covered by virgin timber until 1891. A fire in 1903 burned the north and west sides of the mountain and a portion of the summit to the east. The fire of 1912 burned the eastern slopes down to Long and Black ponds, but the forests on top the eskers have really recovered and provide a lovely setting for the walk along the trail.

The best way to enjoy the ponds is from a canoe or on skis when the ponds are securely frozen. From the middle of the ponds you have tremendous views south to St. Regis Mountain and north to Jenkins Mountain with its imposing cliffs. You will be amazed at the amount of wildlife you will see; a winter ski trip yielded dozens of deer on the ponds and along the road west of Keese Mills.

Debar Mountain Wild Forest

SECLUDED MEACHAM LAKE State Campground in a remote northern Adirondack setting forms the focus of an interesting and diverse assemblage of hikes and cross-country ski jaunts as well as two interesting bushwhacks. All of these trips begin or end at the campground or begin so close to it that the campground can easily serve as a base for exploration of the Debar Mountain Wild Forest.

The campground itself is highlighted by 1200-acre Meacham Lake, one of the larger bodies of water entirely in the Forest Preserve. There is excellent fishing in the lake in spring and summer. The Osgood River is the main inlet of Meacham Lake, while the East Branch of the St. Regis River begins its winding way through northern boreal forests here at the outlet of the lake. Imposing stands of conifers and several attractive natural sand beaches heighten the appeal of the campground. Campground signs are bilingual, attesting to its proximity to Canada and its popularity with urban residents in the Montreal area.

Meacham Lake was discovered by an itinerant hunter-trapper who made his way up the St. Regis River in the early nineteenth century from his native Hopkinton in neighboring St. Lawrence County and erected a crude log shanty on the lakeshore. Thomas Meacham, for whom the lake was named, was credited in his obituary with taking 2550 deer, 210 bear, 77 panthers, and 214 wolves during the course of his life. With such figures it is miraculous that the first two species are still abundant in the area and little wonder that the latter two were entirely eliminated. Today, environmentalists are heartened by reports of cougar and perhaps timber wolves returning to the Adirondacks.

Others were later able to enjoy the wilderness setting at Meacham Lake by staying at one of two large hotels built on its shores. Both were destroyed by fire, the first in 1900 and its replacement in 1921. A short time later, the current state campground came into existence and much of the surrounding land was incorporated into the Forest Preserve, thereby permanently protecting the region's wild quality and making it available to all.

Map XII: Sections 61-67
Based on USGS 7½' non-metric
Lake Titus, Owls Head,
Meacham Lake and Debar Mtn.
Quadrangles

0   ½   1 Mile

– – – Trail
–·–·– Path
········· Bushwhack
Road

14°
Magnetic   True
North   North

Meacham Lake State Campground is on NY 3 and 30. A southern entrance to it is 9.5 miles north of Paul Smiths and a northern entrance is 2.3 miles farther north. The campground is less than 20 miles south of Malone.

This chapter begins with explorations on the northern and western side of the Wild Forest that introduce you to the history of the wild forest area. These routes are accessible from NY 99, which is an east turn from NY 30, 17.4 miles north of Paul Smiths and 13 miles south of Malone.

61 Debar Pond

Trail, fishing
0.3 mile, 5 minutes, level, map XII

This short, marked fishing access trail leads from NY 99 to a lovely, glacial pond. Head east on NY 99 from Duane for 4.25 miles where NY 99 turns abruptly right and becomes more like a country lane than a state highway. Do not miss this turn and do not be tempted to go straight on the wider road. Shortly, another gravel road comes in from the right. Drive south on it for under a mile to a marked DEC parking area on the left. The trailhead is on the right.

The trail heads through a rather wet coniferous swamp on hardwood planks to arrive in 0.3 mile at the pond. Spruce, balsam fir, and the feathery-leaved white cedar, commonly called arbor vitae, fill the swamp. The latter is a favorite winter browse for white-tailed deer in the Adirondacks.

Sharp ridges loom above the pond on both sides; Debar, Loon Lake, and Baldface mountains overshadow it. An attractive private log house sits on a knoll above the pond. This is the site of a many-roomed castle, built by an eccentric German hop baron, Robert Schroeder, who once owned 2100 surrounding acres and the largest hop farm in the area. The house site and the remaining private land around it are slated to become part of the Forest Preserve in the future.

62 Debar Game Management Area

Paths along old roads, hiking, cross-country skiing, hunting, map XII

In the shadow of the twin towers—Debar and Baldface mountains— that loom like sentinels over the surrounding lowlands, lies a maze of interconnecting old tote roads threading through the Forest Preserve land known as the Debar Game Management Area. Comprising 9000 acres, it was once the site of an enclosed elk herd that was to be the nucleus for restoring this imposing cervid to its rightful place among the fauna in the park. The experiment, begun in the 1930s, was suspended, and the elk disappeared by the 1960s. The elk had reproduced and were becoming established, but were eliminated by illegal hunting.

The game management area was set up primarily to enhance and propagate all wildlife species and towards this end artificial ponds and wetlands were created and various silvacultural programs were undertaken to diversify vegetation and hence wildife habitat. The old wire fences used to contain the elk, various open ponds and wetlands, a number of conifer plantations, and especially the network of old roads remain today as a legacy of this era of Forest Preserve management. These roads may be combined for a series of interesting loops and side paths or for one long through trek that connects the game management area with the Meacham Lake State Campground.

To reach the start of the trails, take NY 99, see section 61, east past the turn to Debar Pond for nearly another 4 miles until you see a gravel road on the right, near a small creek with a modest bridge abutment.

Turn west on the gravel road and drive along it, carefully, for 1.3 miles to the beginning of the old Debar Game Management Area. Drive a little farther, 1.2 miles, with care through open fields that were once pastures for grazing elk. This takes you to the spot where three adjacent tote roads head off into emerging woodlands. Park here and start your jaunt, as further travel can only be accomplished with four-wheel drive. Three trails radiate from this point; the first, leading back to Meacham Lake Campground, can obviously be started from there, to end at this point. It is, however, described from east to west.

63 Debar Game Management Area to Meacham Lake Campground

Hiking, hunting, cross-country skiing
7.9 miles, 4 hours, relatively level, map XII

Take the middle trail in the field described in section 62 and you will reach the campground after an easy walk through rolling terrain. It is sporadically marked as a snowmobile or horse trail, but is essentially a wide, woods road. The route lends itself to cross-country skiing, but since neither the campground roads nor the game management area road is plowed in winter, the one-way distance becomes 11.4 miles.

You head south of west and cross several creeks and wetlands near the beginning, all of which drain south into Hatch Brook. You will also see pine plantations, gravel pits, and old foundations. After fifteen minutes, the right hand road in the field enters from the north.

On the left at 1.5 miles, there is a small pond constructed for the wildlife management area. In addition to the dam, water control structures are still visible. The trail continues another 0.5 mile where a grassy tote road comes in on an oblique angle from the east (your left). You go straight.

After another 1.5 miles of mostly level hiking, the trail reaches a "Y." The right fork is the one you want. The clearer trail to the left is the beginning of the Hays Brook Wetland Trail. This point is 3.5 miles from the field, 5.5 miles from NY 99 if you are skiing.

The trail to the right leads over several ridges and meandering creeks flowing through narrow wetlands. At about 4 miles, you reach the take-off point for the bushwhack around East and Star mountains, section 69. It is right after the first of two small corduroy bridges. Your route leads you over several moderate ascents and descents through forests of medium sized hardwoods, interspersed with beaver flows that may be somewhat tricky on skis.

At 6 miles you reach the red-marked trail to Debar Mountain and shortly afterwards the extensive wetlands of what was once Winnebago Pond. At 7.4 miles the hiking trail ends at the site of an old gravel pit that precedes a gate barring vehicular traffic. From here it is 0.5 mile down the road to the the campsites; and in winter another mile to the campground's northern entrance on NY 30 or 2.5 miles to the southern entrance. Since the campground roads are unplowed in winter, even adding the shorter distance plus the 2.5 miles to the field makes the winter through trek 11.4 miles long.

64 Hays Brook Wetland
Path along an old road, maps XII and XIII

This short side path leads to an interesting wetland on the upper reaches of Hays Brook that is a deer yarding area in winter. Take the left fork 3 miles from the field along the route of section 63. The mostly level route descends slightly to terminate 0.9 mile south at a spot where an old log cabin perched at the edge of the wetland slowly crumbles into oblivion under the jagged spine of Sable Mountain. The building was formerly used as the cabin for the fire observer who manned the tower standing on Long Lake Mountain.

From here you can make short explorations into the wetland. Alders border the creek, cardinal flowers bloom on its banks, and tamarack rise from the wetland.

65 Hatch Brook Loop
Path, map XII

A 4.5-mile loop, suitable for hiking only, starts along the left hand tote road, but returns via the middle route of section 63. Blowdown limits its usefulness as a ski trail.

Take a left at the beginning of section 63 and head south. Five minutes from the start, you cross Hatch Brook on a bridge in the midst of its extensive wetlands. The purplish flowers of Joe Pye weed attract insects here in August. The road now leads up over a ridge with sugar maple and beech, and it is here that the route is most obstructed by noble specimens of the latter species.

Turn west and at 1.8 miles pass one of the longer artificial impoundments of the game management projects. At 2.5 miles you reach the trail to Meacham Lake. You turn right, east, completing the loop by passing several creeks, another man-made pond, and an extensive pine plantation.

66 Debar Mountain

Hiking, views, lean-to
3.7 miles, 2 hours, 1600-foot vertical rise, map XII

Dominating Meacham Lake Campground and the surrounding area is the imposing mass of Debar Mountain. Its summit, like the summits of St. Regis and Azure mountains, was deliberately cleared by Verplanck Colvin's survey crews in his attempt to triangulate the northern region. At the end of October 1877, his party reached the mountain, whose "summit was peculiar with a steep cliff facing the west, over which the axemen soon commenced to fell the trees obstructing the view. Hanging for a moment on the verge, they would bend slowly over, to plunge with a sudden spring downward, and woe to any thing that should be caught by the splintered butt, as it flew upward with a sudden resistless spring before the plunge. . . . This front was quickly cleared, and the axemen worked lanes eastward and northward through the timber. . . . But telescope was needless to show the grand features of the scene below. Glittering lakes, set in a forest of emerald evergreen, or margined with tamaracks, still clad in the golden foliage of fall, shone far and near. Wild mountain masses rose in dark tumultuous billows eastward, where Whiteface, capped with snow, gleamed in Alpine grandeur. Still further northward the flattened crest and clustering lower peaks of Lyon mountain (densely forest covered from foot to crown) stretched across the horizon, an obstacle to vision; then the rocky front of Owl's Head. . . North-westward stretched the vast plains of Canada, and clearly defined between a breadth of dark blue water, like a great band from west to east, showed the St. Lawrence, the father of the northern river."

The mountain was named for John Debar, a native of Quebec, who was another guide and hunter of renown in the middle of the last century.

From the entrance to Meacham Lake Campground, it is 0.5 mile to campsite #48. Take the dirt road just west of the campsite, staying right, for 0.5 mile to a sand pit where the trail begins at a gated snowmobile barrier. It is a mostly level walk along an old tote road past the gravel pit for 1 mile to the large wetland that borders a tributary of Winnebago Brook. Winnebago Pond, to the south, shown larger on old maps, is now more wetland than water. You cross the wetland surrounding the tributary and at 1.1 miles take the red-marked trail to the left, leaving the old tote road that continues straight ahead. The latter passes Winnebago Pond and leads to the Game Management area, section 63.

After 5 minutes of walking, the trail begins to rise imperceptibly through a hardwood forest. At about 2.7 miles, you cross a shoulder between the twin goliaths of Black and Debar mountains. The grade continues relatively easy until at 3.2 miles you reach a field with a DEC lean-to and the remains of the old fire observer's cabin just beyond. The lean-to has been vandalized, but is still serviceable.

From here on it is all steep—as steep as any fire tower trail. Stairs have been built into the hillside, bare rock and talus make the going slow. In 0.5 mile, you climb 800 feet and reach the summit out of breath for sure.

With the tower gone, you have to search around the summit to find the best vantages, for in spite of Colvin's clearing, the summit is recovering. Turn right off the main trail just before the summit to one which looks south toward the High Peaks, including Algonquin and Marcy. Meacham Lake Campground and Clear Pond are clearly etched below the mountain. In the far northwest lies the Deer River Flow, recently acquired by DEC. By moving about, you can find vantages that offer much of Colvin's prospect.

67 Baldface Mountain
Bushwhack, map XII

One spring day eighty or so years ago, Charles Stickney set up a tent and tethered a cow in the middle of nowhere. More precisely, he was somewhere on Baldface Mountain, probably the lower southern slopes above what later became the State Game Management Area.

Charles was in his late teens, and he had tuberculosis. He came to Baldface to follow the regimen of Dr. Edward Livingston Trudeau's fresh-air cure. The philosophy behind the cure was that prolonged rest, plenty of wholesome food, peace of mind, and at least eight hours a day in fresh air would aid the body in fighting the disease. Taking the air was usually done on a porch or veranda, but some people lived in tents (even the tents often had porches). Charles spent winters at the Stickney homestead south of Loon Lake; but, after the April thaw, he headed north to Baldface, where he stayed till stormy November forced him home. It took him three years (about the average) to recover from the illness, which, before Trudeau's time, had almost always been fatal.

Though Charles Stickney spent the rest of his long life hunting and trapping in the area, his compact, steep, bare-headed mountain never acquired his name, nor did it acquire a trail. You have a superb view of Baldface from the south from the meadows of the Game Management Area, but the best way to climb it is from the northeast.

Follow NY 99 east, being sure to turn right at 4.25 miles, and drive another 2.3 miles and park. Small cars are recommended for the road is very narrow and has almost no shoulders. There is an unnamed intermittent stream flowing from the west. Where it flows under the road, there are some wooden guardposts: three on the west side of the road and four on the east. Just south of this point the road makes a sharp left turn. All these details should keep you from parking at the wrong stream if your odometer differs from the guide's mileage.

Begin bushwhacking where the stream goes under the road, following a compass bearing of 221° from true north, 236° magnetic. After an initial steep pitch, the grade is moderate, but gradually steepens again as you climb. The forest is mature hardwood, and some of the trees are very large. At 320 yards above the road, there is a yellow birch with a chest-high girth of 12.25 feet. That's big!

On this part of the mountain you will be pushing through stands of wood or horse nettle, which can be as much as four feet high. Wood nettle is a relatively mild cousin of the infamous stinging nettle. Both plants sting in the same way. They are armed with tiny, brittle, hollow hairs loaded with histamines and other irritants. When touched, the hairs break off like little glass tubes, piercing the skin and injecting their venom. It is wise to wear long pants and long sleeved shirts here.

Growing among the wood nettles is a profusion of touch-me-not or jewel weed. What you see here is not the familiar orange flowered type, but a larger, yellow variety that is fond of rich soils. Mashed jewelweed leaves are a folk remedy for nettle stings, and the two are frequently found conveniently growing together.

Above the big birch tree the grade becomes very steep until you reach a wall-like cliff at 370 yards. Turn left and follow the base of the wall on moderate to steep grades. At about 445 yards, you will come to a break. Turn right, climb up through the break, and resume your original bearing (221° true). You encounter a taller wall at 535 yards. Turn left and follow its base. The grade along this cliff is easy, the woods and rocks lovely, and the respite from climbing well earned.

There is a break in the wall at 605 yards. Turn right, go up through the break, and again follow the 221° bearing. The climbing in and just above the break is steep, but soon moderates and remains moderate in second

Looking northwest from Baldface over Debar Pond toward the Deer River Flow

growth hardwoods all the way to the crest of the mountain's north ridge at 765 yards.

If your orienteering matches the guide's, you will hit the crest at its only level area. Turn left and follow the crest (rather wide here but narrowing above), first on the level (even down a bit) and then climbing in alternating easy and moderate stretches. At 1135 yards, the grade becomes moderate to moderately steep. You reach a transverse ledge at 1255 yards. Go around it to the right; and loop back left, returning to the ridge crest at 1320 yards. This detour offers the last moderate to steep climbing. The grades from here on are mostly easy with a few moderate pitches.

All the way along the ridge, the forest has become increasingly dominated by paper birches, which now become noticeably shorter and more closely spaced. At 1530 yards, there is a small open patch, and, at 1580 yards, you will push through the scrub and emerge onto the bare summit, 2867 feet above sea level, 1065 feet above your starting point. The 1580-yard bushwhack computes to 0.9 mile and should take no more than an hour and a half.

A subsidiary summit lies 85 yards to the south. Combining the two summits, you will have one of the finest panoramas in the northern Adirondacks. Especially striking are the views of Debar Pond and Mountain to the west and Hatch Brook Valley backed by Loon Lake Mountain and Sable Mountains to the south with the Game Management Area at your feet. Other interesting prospects are northwest toward Deer River Flow and Lake Titus, north through the cap cut by the Salmon River between Titusville Mountain and Owls Head toward the flatlands of the St. Lawrence Valley, and southeast over Duck Pond and Loon Lake toward the Wilmington Range and Whiteface.

Of course, there is much more, and naming unfamiliar mountains from an even less familiar perspective is challenging fun. You can spend a lot of time on this summit, but eventually you will have to come down. Here is an alternative route.

Descend as you ascended, along the ridge crest, for 820 yards, to the level section where you intersected the crest on your way up. Now, instead of turning right and heading down the flank, continue down the ridge crest. The grade at first is easy, and then becomes moderate; but, at 985 yards from the summit, it becomes moderately steep and steep. It stays that way until abruptly easing at 1350 yards at the edge of a saddle. The descent is gentle to the bottom of the saddle at 1430 yards. Turn right and follow the drainage down mostly easy grades. At 1560 yards, you reach the head of a stream that will guide you to NY 99 and your starting point. The descent is 60 yards short of a mile this way.

68   Hays Brook Truck Trail to Sheep Meadow

Snowmobile and horse trail, hiking, cross-country skiing
3.6 miles, 1½ hours, level, maps XI and XIII

For a relatively level trail that offers both an excellent cross-country ski jaunt and an interesting hike through diverse conifer plantations and boreal habitat, look no further. To find the trailhead, drive 3.7 miles north on NY 30 from Paul Smith's College, which is at the intersection of NY 30 and 192. Here a DEC sign reading "Hays Brook Assembly Area" marks a road to the right, east. Follow it for 0.5 mile to the gate that marks the beginning of the trail. (Though the USGS spells it Hays, local custom and history seem to favor Hayes. For consistency, this guide uses Hays.)

The trail crosses both the Osgood River and Hays Brook, famous fishing streams that were the major attractions for fishermen who stayed at McCollums, a hotel that stood along the present NY 30. A hotel built there around 1850 was replaced by a grand establishment, which too burned in 1924. Even the original hotel was built on burned lands and 6000 acres surrounding McCollums were burned in the great fire of 1908. The trail traverses these lands.

From the gate, walk northeast for 0.3 mile to a short spur, which forks right. If you turn here, a twenty-minute, 1-mile walk along a path following an old road takes you through a majestic evergreen canopy to a point upriver on the Osgood, which is the site of one of the tent platforms, once so common in the area.

A ten-minute walk on the main trail, 0.3 mile, takes you to a rustic bridge over the Osgood River. Immediately after crossing the Osgood, the Hays Brook Trail turns sharply left, while the truck trail continues straight ahead (the trail rejoins it later). Just ahead on the truck trail to the right, another spur trail heads east for 1.4 miles to Grass Pond, a tiny, grassy-shored body of water that is surrounded by private land.

The main trail to the left begins a gradual rise through an impressive evergreen plantation of Scotch, red, and white pine. The trail leads through the plantation for a mile, and if you are walking in early spring, watch for the blossoms of the trailing arbutus. Wildlife is limited due to the monoculture, but the symmetry and aroma of the pines help compensate for the loss. All of this area had to be reforested after the disastrous fire of 1908.

At 1.3 miles, The Hays Brook Trail rejoins the truck trail and shortly thereafter, at 1.5 miles, crosses Hays Brook on another wooden bridge.

Horse barn near the Old Sheep Meadow

Another forty-five minutes of easy walking through rolling, sandy terrain, brings you to an old sheep meadow, at 3.6 miles. It is a charming, secluded vista, of low mountains surrounding the meadow, which is rapidly filling with black cherry and red spruce. At the far side of the clearing are two lean-tos and a run down horse shelter. Used relatively little today, this pastoral setting with its natural reforestation contrasts vividly with man induced plantations nearby.

69 Around East Mountain
Bushwhack, map XIII

A long, but interesting trek takes you from the Old Sheep Meadow on the Hays Brook Trail, section 68, over the shoulder of Star Mountain, east between Square Mountain and Little Cherry Hill, north around private land, and over a shoulder of East Mountain to intersect the trail from Meacham Lake to the Debar Game Management Area. From here a left turn will take you back to the Meacham Lake Campground in 3.1 miles. If you spot a vehicle here, the through trek from the Hays Brook Trailhead will be 13.5 miles.

Although described as a cross-country ski trip in some guides, this trail is best considered a bushwhack for the markers are sporadic and in the last decade there has been considerable blowdown, obscuring the trail in places. Perhaps a semi-bushwhack more accurately describes this trip.

Mileage is given from Old Sheep Meadow, 3.6 miles. Follow the roadway north through the meadow. At 4.2 miles a path with occasional markers continues east over rolling terrain. At 5.2 miles, the path has curved to the east and begins to rise, passing between two of the low mountains, Square and Cherry Hill.

At 2.9 miles, more than an hour and a half of leisurely walking, watching closely to stay on the route, you reach a sliver of private land. Because this is posted against trespass by paper company leaseholders, you must follow the boundary markers around the perimeter of the private land until you reach the path again. The boundary heads north for 1.6 miles, then turns east. At this point, you contour northeast on level grade around the slopes of East Mountain, where you should pick up the path again. Once you return to it, the path descends in a northerly direction from the shoulder of East Mountain to cross a long stretch of spruce flats. The going can be wet. Finally, after 6.7 miles of mixed hiking and semi-bushwhacking, following indistinct markers, past the Old Sheep Meadow, you reach the trail of section 63. A left turn on it takes you to Meacham Lake Campground in an hour of easy walking.

70 Slush Pond

Cross-country skiing on an unplowed road
5.0 miles round trip, 3 hours, level, maps XI and XIII

A road, usually unplowed in winter, leads through Forest Preserve Land to Slush Pond. You can ski it as far as the gate of a large private park that lies to the west of the pond. The road begins on NY 30, 3.7 miles north of Paul Smith's at the intersection of NY 30 and 192.

The road is generally level as it heads west through an impressive mixed plantation of scotch and white pine. At 2 miles you can see Slush Pond, a small boreal bond encircled by sedges, then a ring of alder, spruce, and tamarack swamp. There are several primitive campsites in the vicinity of the pond, but in summer, you can drive to them even though the pond and surrounding land is in the Forest Preserve. The gate at 2.5 miles is as far west as you can ski.

For variety you can ski a mile or so along an old logging road that circles from the end of the road around to the south and back north to intersect the road again near the shores of Slush Pond. Another road branches north not far from the beginning. It heads downhill and passes some lovely marshes before reaching a hunting camp. It too could serve to vary a ski trip along the road to Slush Pond.

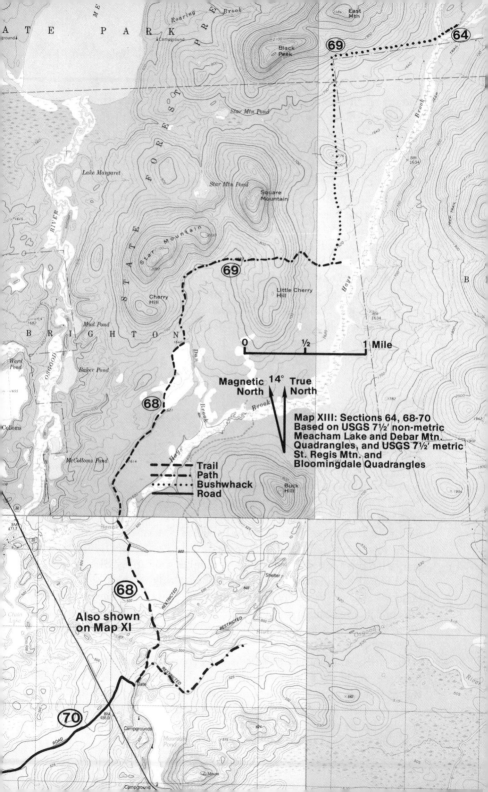

Map XIII: Sections 64, 68-70
Based on USGS 7½′ non-metric
Meacham Lake and Debar Mtn.
Quadrangles, and USGS 7½′ metric
St. Regis Mtn. and
Bloomingdale Quadrangles

Magnetic North 14° True North

0   ½   1 Mile

Trail
Path
Bushwhack
Road

Also shown
on Map XI

Kate Mountain and Little Haystack

KATE MOUNTAIN IS actually a group of small mountains and large hills north of the hamlet of Vermontville in the southern part of the Town of Franklin in Franklin County. If you are traveling north from Vermontville on NY 3, the east and west peaks of this group dominate the landscape. The west peak is the highest, with a summit elevation of 2841 feet. The summit is mostly wooded, but there are ledges and cliffs on its south rim and east and west ends that offer excellent views.

The mountain's name as spelled by the USGS is incorrect. It was originally called "Cate" after a family that settled on its lower northeast slopes around 1829.

Kate Mountain is part of what geologists call an overturned anticline. An anticline is an upfold in the earth's crust. Sit on your bed and push the blankets together from each side until you get a long hump. That is an anticline. Now, push the hump over on its side. That is an overturned anticline. Most of the Kate Mountain anticline is made of Loon Lake syenite—a rock similar to granite but containing less quartz. It is very hard and quite attractive, with its minerals often arranged in patterns of wavy lines—a result of the pressures of mountain building.

There are many ways to approach the west peak of Kate Mountain. Two of the more direct are from the Sinkhole Road on the southeast side and County Route 30 on the north side. Even though you reach it via NY 3, you may want to take a small detour to the east. Just north of Bloomingdale, turn right on Fletcher Farm Road, then north on Norman Ridge, which will take you back to NY 3 at Vermontville. From Norman Ridge you have a good view of Kate as well as views to the south across the Saranac River to the north slopes of the McKenzie Wilderness and southeast to Whiteface. Norman Ridge is a high plateau, formed of glacial silt and fine sands, where potatoes are raised. Along the roadside you will see snow buntings, bluebirds, and sharp shinned, cooper's, and broad winged hawks as well as kestrals. The birds of prey often sit quite still on the utility wires beside the road.

71 Kate from the North

Bushwhack, map XIV

This is a lovely way to go up the mountain. It is less difficult than the southern route and is even easier in winter when the gentler grades make it possible to snowshoe or ski over low-level obstructions.

Follow NY 3 north from the Franklin Town Hall in Vermontville for 5 miles to County Route 30. Turn left and proceed a little over 2 miles west on this road and park. You should be at or near a culvert through which a stream flows from the south. It may be dry in late summer, but its bed is obvious. This is the uppermost section of Negro Brook, the longest stream entirely within the Town of Franklin. For most of its length it is a dark, twisting, slow-moving but powerful, swamp-fed little river of the lowlands; but, above County Route 30, it is a bright and straight-forward mountain brook. Follow it upstream.

There is very little climbing to do for the first 1020 yards, which will bring you to the mouth of a small but interesting gorge.

When Kate Mountain was formed, a stray lens of Grenville metasediment, nearly a mile long but only about 100 yards wide at the present surface, got folded into the mass of Loon Lake syenite that comprises most of the mountain. Where the metasediments—here mostly reddish quartzite and blackish-green amphibolite—and the syenite contact, there is a zone of weakness. For about 230 yards, the course of Negro Brook coincides with this zone of weakness at a place where the mountain steepens. Hence the gorge. To the east is the Grenville rock; to the west is the firmer and slightly younger syenite. During low water, you can climb right up through the gorge; and, at, at least, one spot in the streambed, you can see where these two very different rock types actually make contact.

Above the gorge, there is a very pretty dell. A steep climb east from here will bring you to the bald north summit of Kate's east peak. Though the views south and west are dominated by the rest of the Kate group, the views north and east are far-reaching and impressive.

To reach the west peak, continue up Negro Brook. From the dell to the saddle between the east and west peaks it is about 640 yards. The ascent is easy to moderate all the way. The forest, as it has been from the road, is mature hardwoods.

When you reach the height-of-land between the two peaks, turn right and head westerly up the spine of a ridge. Stay as close to the crest as

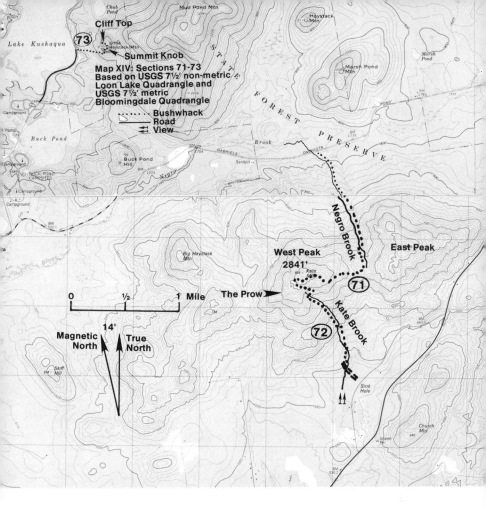

possible. As you climb—first gradually, then more and more steeply—you will find that this ridge becomes broader rather than narrower as you gain altitude, and its crest becomes harder to divine, but it tends to be south of center.

Eventually, you will begin to encounter open patches, and then a very steep pitch of bare rock. The top of this pitch marks the eastern end of the summit ridge and is about 1225 yards from the saddle. There are views from east to south and an especially interesting view of Loon Lake and surrounding mountains to the north.

Follow the ledge west. In 30 yards you will come to a slight dip, and in 65 yards, a much wider and deeper one. Beyond this second dip you will see another, higher patch of open rock. That is the summit ledge, about 160 yards away. Your total distance will be 1.9 miles with an elevation gain of 1080 feet. Allow two and a half hours for the climb.

Your reward is a 200° vista that includes, from northeast to southwest, Silver Lake Mountain, Union Falls Lake, Mount Mansfield, Catamount, Esther and Whiteface, the McKenzie Range, a selection of High Peaks from Dix to Seward, Ampersand Mountain, Mount Morris, and St. Regis Mountain along the horizon with Vermontville and its surrounding farmlands below.

For a little more effort, however, you will be as well rewarded again. The top of Kate Mountain is very wide where it is highest, but it tapers westward like the prow of a ship. Follow the southern rim of the mountain top southwest and west over numerous bumps. You will lose some altitude along the way, but no more than about 60 feet, though the ups and downs make the loss seem greater. After about fifteen or twenty minutes, you come out on west-facing ledges where the mountain drops away very abruptly. You may have been lucky enough to hit the tip of the prow itself. If not, look around a while until you find it. It is the top of a 200-foot cliff liberally marked with raven droppings. This is a raven elevator. The prevailing winds slam into the cliff, creating a nearly permanent updraft. The birds ride it to about 60 to 100 feet above the cliff top, get off, cruise around the mountain, get back on the draft near the bottom, and ride it up again.

The ravens are great to watch, and the view is superb—an unobstructed panorama from the Seward Range in the south to Loon Lake in the north.

72 Kate from the South
Bushwhack, map XIV

The southern route up Kate Mountain is shorter and rougher than the northern one and involves an 1140-foot elevation gain in just under a mile. Allow two hours for a one-way trip to the summit.

Drive north on NY 3 from the Franklin Town Hall 1.6 miles to the south end of Sinkhole Road. Turn left, drive another 0.7 mile and park. This should put you opposite the beginning of an old tote road known by some as the Chair Road. If there were a trail, this would be the trailhead; but there are no trails up Kate Mountain.

Walk along the Chair Road about 140 yards through a Norway Spruce plantation to Kate Brook (the first brook you will see). Turn right and follow the brook upstream. It will be your guide much of the way up the

Vermontville and the potato fields of Norman Ridge from the summit of Kate Mountain, the McKenzie Range in the background

mountain, but you will not find it (let alone its tributaries) on your map because the USGS ignored about nine out of ten streams in this part of the Adirondacks.

As you ascend very gently along Kate Brook, you pass the mouths of three tributaries: first, Zephyr Brook that comes in from your right; then Yoohoo Brook that comes in from your left; and about 325 yards above Chair Road, Ginger Brook, also coming in from your left. These are all quite small, and you may not even notice them, especially around summer's end, when all these streams tend to dry up. Even in the most parched of times, though, Ginger continues to discharge a trickle of water into Kate, which itself may be dry above that point. So to avoid being led astray, follow the larger stream, even if there is no water in it.

The grade continues to be gentle in a hardwood forest, though the brook's bed gradually becomes deeper until, at approximately 525 yards, the slope steepens noticeably and the stream flows in a true ravine. At 715 yards, the grade steepens still more, but it eases at 820 yards, and the ravine widens.

Climbing becomes steeper again at 890 yards. The brook flows around an interesting rock knob at 925 yards; and, at 1000 yards, it splits into multiple channels. The grade eases again at 1045 yards. Here, a tributary enters from the right; and, farther off to the right, you can see ledges. Follow the left channel.

For the past 520 yards, the climbing has been mostly moderate to moderately steep with only a few steeper pitches. At 1150 yards, the grade becomes downright easy among widely spaced, mature hardwoods. It is a pleasant surprise so high up on the mountain and would make for a fine stroll except that there is an understory growing thicker than the quills on a porcupine's tail. Stay close to the stream. You do not want to lose it now!

The stream splits at just under 1230 yards. Follow the left fork. It breaks up and disappears under rock jumble as the grade gets steeper at 1255 yards. Pretend it is still visible and continue northwesterly. At 1300 yards, it redefines only to go under rocks again at 1330 yards. Climb about 14 yards more into the rubble and stop.

Look to your right, bearing 18° to 20° east of true north. You should see evidence of ledges through the trees. Summer's thick foliage may make this difficult, but have faith. Follow this bearing for about 85 yards not allowing yourself to be diverted significantly by any small, intervening ledges, and you come to the base of a line of cliffs and ledges that runs northwesterly (to your left) all the way to the top of the mountain.

Now you have a choice. You can try to find a "safe" route to the top of the cliffs and thread patches of open ledges to the summit, or you can work your way up along the base of the cliffs through intervals of thickets and blowdowns, 275 yards to the head of a ravine just west of the summit. The grades are mostly moderate to steep. Turn north and climb steeply about 25 yards to the ridge crest. Then hook to the right, easterly and southeasterly, for an additional 90, nearly level, yards to reach the south-facing ledge.

73 Little Haystack
Bushwhack, map XIV

Little Haystack is not quite the smallest mountain described in this book, but it lives up to the saying, good things come in small packages. In fact, this is a perfect package for a morning or afternoon picnic or outing, especially for people staying at Buck Pond State Campground and looking for something a bit different to do.

Access is from the campground, off Franklin County Route 30 just east of the hamlet of Onchiota and 5 miles west of NY 3. The main campground road runs roughly north-south. At its northern end, it makes a sharp right turn and then ends at the Buck Pond Beach parking lot. Exactly at the curve, an unpaved road continues north. Follow this road for 0.66 mile.

This is the old bed of the Delaware and Hudson Railroad. Lake Kushaqua is on your left with views toward Loon Lake Mountain. Eventually you pass a mile post that reads "59" on one side and "24" on the other: 59 miles to the main line in Plattsburgh and 24 miles to the terminus in Lake Placid.

At about 0.57 mile, you come to a small pond along side the railroad bed on the right. Turn right and enter the woods, climbing up a short, moderately steep slope. Then, following a compass bearing of about 5° south of true east, 120° magnetic, proceed on a mostly easy slope through a hardwood forest with a liberal admixture of conifers. There will be a drainage to your right, south, where evergreens predominate. Try to stay along the rim of this if it cuts across your line of compass orientation. Then pick up your bearing again when the rim of the drainage begins to trend more southerly.

After gradually ascending, the slope will increase to moderate at 215 yards. At 320 yards from the railroad bed, the slope abruptly steepens, and, at 435 yards, you encounter ledges. Stay to their right, following a route that climbs and hugs the base of the ledges as closely as possible. They will be broken at about 520 yards by a shallow and very steep draw—a chute, really—a route almost directly to the summit.

Turn left and ascend the chute. The grade is very steep at first, but becomes extremely steep before leveling off at the top at 595 yards. The summit knob is nearby to your right. You can climb onto it either from the west or east sides. The bushwhack is no more than 660 yards. Add that to your walk along the railroad grade, and you have walked but 1.05 miles, 2.3 miles from County Route 30. Summit altitude is 2101 feet above sea level for a total ascent of 420 feet.

That really is not much of a mountain, but sometimes a low summit has special advantages. When fog shrouds higher mountains, Little Haystack may remain below the concealing clouds. Then, you can look outward from Kate Mountain in the southeast to Azure Mountain in the west, and down to Buck Pond, Kushaqua Narrows, Lake Kushaqua, Chub Pond, and the north end of Rainbow Lake, and the North Branch of the Saranac River.

The view from the summit knob is primarily southward, but a short walk will bring you to the brink of a cliff with prospects toward the west and northwest.

From the knob, bushwhack along the ridgecrest to where it begins to lose definition and drop off at 170 yards. From here, loop around to the left, descending moderately to steeply through conifers (in places quite thick) to the edge of the cliff at 240 yards. Be careful. There are lots of places to twist an ankle, and the cliff has no real threshold. You may find yourself pushing down through scrubby spruce and suddenly there is nothing in front of you but empty space. There is a small, downward-slanting ledge you can sit on. It is about thirty inches wide. Stay off it unless it is dry. The cliff is vertical and even overhangs a bit, and it is 200 feet to the bottom. The view from this spot is superb. At your feet is almost all of Lake Kushaqua. Chub Pond is off to the right, and the Loon Lake Mountains form an impressive backdrop.

Much of the land you see once belonged to the White Fathers of Africa, a Roman Catholic missionary order that bought the impressive facilities of Stoney Wold Sanatorium in the 1950s and sold most of it to the state in the 1970s. The state destroyed the huge, Elizabethan Revival main building and adjoining laundry and power plant leaving the chapel and two large cottages intact. The Stoney Wold Depot on the old New York

View of south end of Lake Kushaqua from the west cliff of Little Haystack

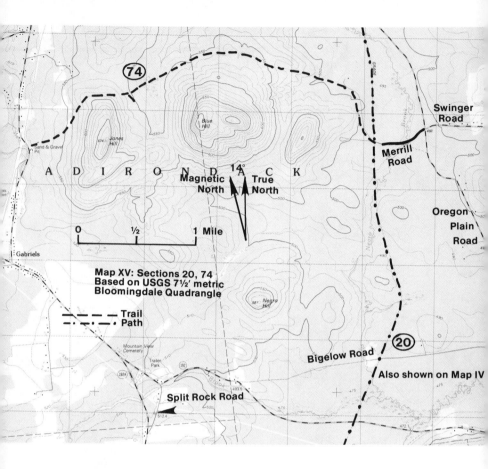

Map XV: Sections 20, 74
Based on USGS 7½' metric
Bloomingdale Quadrangle

Trail
Path

Central line was moved to Merrillsville. The remaining buildings are now in private hands. The softball field will soon be woods again.

Stoney Wold was one of many large institutions—nearly self-contained, self-sustaining communities—that were built to house people who came to the Saranac Lake area to undertake the fresh-air and bed-rest cure for tuberculosis. In 1901, when Stoney Wold was incorporated, there were 30,000 people with tuberculosis in the tenement districts of New York City alone and only five sanatoria in the entire state to care for people stricken by the White Plague.

Stoney Wold itself was founded by Elizabeth W. Newcomb, the wife of a successful New York City physician, for the express purpose of providing care for self-supporting young women, young married women, and little children in the early stages of the disease. Almost all the donators of funds for purchase of land and construction of buildings were women. The incorporators consisted of fourteen women and fifteen men. There were nine officers, and all but the treasurer were women; and all the directors were women.

Mrs. Newcomb studied many localities for her sanatorium, and the best she found consisted of 1250 acres about 3 miles north of Onchiota. On the property were a number of structures, including a power plant and a hotel. The acreage included Buck Pond, part of Mountain Pond, all of Lake Kushaqua, and the mountain upon which you stand. The purchase price was $20,000.

To get back down the mountain, you can either retrace your steps or you can head straight for the lake, after circumventing the cliff top. If you choose the latter course, you can go left or right. If you go left and down, the terrain is trickier, and there is a greater likelihood of becoming cliff-hung—proof that you can have an adventure on even the smallest of mountains. If you go to the right and down, the descent is very steep at first. Then you cross undulating ground in a beautiful, mature hardwood forest. One way or another, you eventually come to the old D & H right-of-way. You would have to work hard to get lost here.

74 Around Jones and Blue Hills

Snowmobile trail, cross-country sking
3.5 miles, 2 hours, 400-foot elevation change, map XV

A snowmobile trail following dirt roads connects Oregon Plains Road with the road from Gabriels to Rainbow Lake. Snowmobilers use it just enough to keep a good, packed surface suitable for skiers, who must of course watch out for the machines. The scrubby second growth makes the trail less attractive in other seasons, so the area is used mostly by hunters. The trail traverses two patches of private land over which the state has easements.

The western trailhead is at a gravel pit opposite Jones Pond. The eastern trailhead is Merrill Road, a left turn from Oregon Plains Road opposite Swinyer Road. This intersection can be reached from Bloomingdale or Vermontville easily. Merrill Road, access to the northern end of the bogs described in section 20, is not plowed in winter, so park along Oregon Plains Road.

DEC signs mark the trail. Go west for 0.3 mile over the railroad embankment and 100 feet beyond turn right, northwest, across an abandoned field into young mixed growth woods. The trail gradually rises on the northern slopes of Blue Hill, swings around the hill and dips to the southwest. Then it turns northeast to make a similar circuit of the north slopes of Jones Hill. The descent from the slopes of Jones Hill contain the only slopes steep enough to be considered intermediate. Here you encounter 200 yards of narrow, winding schuss. The rest is gentle and not demanding.

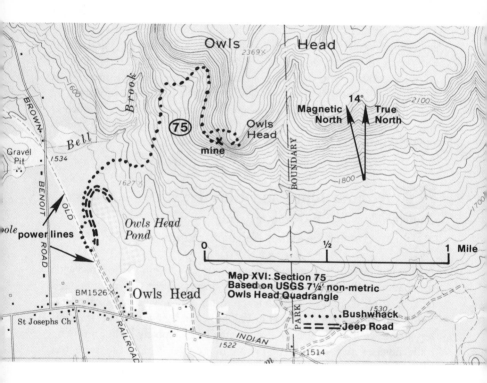

Near Titusville and Owls Head

WHILE THE LOWLANDS north of the Adirondacks were being settled in the early decades of the nineteenth century, the Great South Woods provoked fear and were left alone, much as the North Woods were untouched by early settlers on the southern fringes of the Adirondack Mountains. Daniel McCormack divided Alexander McComb's great purchase (of 3,693,755 acres) in St. Lawrence and Franklin counties in thirds. By 1830, Henry B. Titus had acquired the southern two-thirds of this tract, where there were at that time no settlements. He founded Titusville, establishing a sawmill and a gristmill, but the community failed because there were no roads to take the timber and iron to market.

In 1850, the Northern Railroad was completed, and the community sprang to life. Mills along Branch Brook, the outlet of Lake Titus, and along the Salmon River to the east sent lumber north and east to Lake Champlain.

75 Owls Head Mountain
Unmarked path, hiking, views, map XVI

When the night train on the Adirondack Division of the New York Central stopped at Owls Head on still winter evenings, the depot thermometer consistently displayed the coldest reading on the line. That is why this hamlet ten miles south of Malone became known as the "ice box of New York." The view from the summit of Owls Head Mountain shows why the little community is so frosty. It is situated on the floor of a high basin (elevation 1526 feet) with mountains ringing it all around—a perfect place for cold air to settle.

There are more than a few Owls Head mountains within the Blue Line. This one is the farthest north, just inside the park in the Town of Belmont, and was Colvin's key triangulation peak between Lyon Mountain and St. Regis. From a distance, it gives the impression of a rather ordinary ridge, but from a nearer perspective, a 300-foot cliff is revealed, and the view from the cliff is extraordinary indeed.

The path up this Owls Head of the north is unmarked and unmaintained, but it is so well traveled and defined that following it is no problem. All of it is on private land, so please respect it as you would your own to assure continued access.

To get to the path-head, drive east on NY 99 from its intersection with NY 30. At 4.2 miles, NY 99 takes a turn to the right, and County Route 27 continues straight ahead. Follow county Route 27 a distance of 9.2 miles (total from NY 30, 13.4 miles) to Owls Head hamlet. Turn right and drive 0.25 mile down Owls Head's main street. Pass Wood's Country Store. Immediately after crossing under power lines that follow the old railroad grade, turn left onto a side street that ends in 0.25 mile at a small farm. Park on the shoulder of the road. The powerlines are to your left. To your right is an excellent view of your objective, the great cliff of Owls Head Mountain.

Begin walking northbound along the powerlines. Proceed about 285 yards to a point just past a second set of poles. To your right, you should see a gap in the fence through which a path leads eastward. Follow this path 85 yards to an old woods road. Turn left on the woods road, and walk another 250 yards to an intersection. The woods road continues to the right around Owls Head Pond. Bear left onto a fairly wide trail. This is an old ore road that leads to an abandoned iron mine high up on the mountain. You will follow it on easy and moderate grades for the next 1515 yards.

At 295 yards, there is a short corduroy to cross as the trail begins to climb out of evergreens into hardwoods. The trail splits at 455 yards, soon to reunite. The right fork is muddier than the left. You cross an unmapped, intermittent stream flowing from the right at 615 yards and a year-round stream, also flowing from the right, at 855 yards. This is a lovely spot and a fine place to take a break.

Farther on, at 1215 yards, you cross the headwater run of this brook flowing, when it is not dry, from the left. Then the path traverses the side of the mountain at mostly easy grades until, at 1515 yards, 0.85 mile, about a half hour into the walk, you reach a junction. The junction is not very obvious.

To the left, the land rises steeply, laced with herd paths over wet ledges. Ahead and down to the right, there is what appears to be a small

Looking from Owls Head toward Indian and Mountain View lakes with the Elbow Range
in the distance

overgrown talus slope. This is actually the mine dump, and some interesting mineral specimens can be found among the discarded rocks, including sunstone, a variety of feldspar impregnated with flecks of hemetite (red iron oxide), which sparkles coppery red when held at certain angles under bright light. The trail straight ahead leads shortly to the old mine where the ore is magnetite or black iron oxide.

To reach the top of the cliff, you must go left, up the steep slope. The herd paths soon converge into a true trail. This is the only really steep climbing of the whole hike, and it only lasts for 50 yards. The grade is then moderate for another 45 yards, after which it is moderate to easy.

There is a second junction 240 yards above the old mine road. It is not as obscure as the last one, but it does not exactly jump out at you either. There is a spur path here to the right that leads 65 yards to the apex of the cliff and the best view from the mountain. The path straight ahead continues 75 yards to the northeastern corner of the cliff top. You can make an interesting circuit by combining the two routes, going out on the main trail and then picking your way along the top of the cliff back to the apex and returning to the main trail via the spur path. This is not recommended in wet weather and should not be done in winter. A little patch of ice can lose you a lot of altitude awfully fast. Unless conditions are optimal, use the spur path both coming and going.

The view from the apex of Owls Head cliff is startling in its breadth. So marvelous a span of valley and mountain! It is hard to believe that such an easy walk—1.03 miles with a 675-foot elevation gain—ends with such a generous reward. The vista sweeps from Lyon Mountain in the east to the St. Lawrence Valley in the west-northwest. Between are Whiteface and a stretch of the High Peaks, Indian and Mountain View lakes, the Plumadore Range, the Loon Lake Mountains, the wild heights of Baldface and Debar, the hamlet of Owls Head at your feet, and the long plateau of Titusville Mountain walling the Salmon River Valley to the west. It's easy to spend two or three hours up here and not feel you have stayed too long.

76   Titusville Mountain
Bushwhack, map XVII

Though just outside the Blue Line in the southeastern corner of the Town of Malone, Titusville Mountain is geologically and geographically still part of the Adirondacks. The mountain makes an enticing pattern on the Owls

Head quadrangle. While its contour lines are widely spaced on the north, west, and south, they are packed tightly together on the east, indicating a very steep slope that runs for nearly three miles—a slope that rises as much as 700 feet in as little as 0.3 mile. All you have to do is glance at the map to see there must be cliffs—significant cliffs—on the east side of Titusville Mountain.

Not only are there cliffs, large and small, there are ravines and even a modest canyon. It is a big mountain offering much to explore. What follows is one of a multitude of possibilities.

Turn east from NY 30 on NY 99 and follow it 2.6 miles to a left turn onto Studley Hill Road (Duane Hill Road on the topo map). You pass the intersection with Ayres Road (also unpaved) at 0.8 mile at a cemetery. From a steep downgrade at 3 miles you get your first good view of Titusville Mountain, or at least a portion of it.

At 3.45 miles, the road crosses Townline Brook, giving another view of the mountain. Pavement begins at 4 miles, and at 5.2 miles, a logging road turns off to the left, west. There is a pale blue blaze on a tree at this point as well as blue markings on the pavement. Park here in winter or very wet weather. Just past this spot, Studley Hill Road turns sharply right and then left to meet the Salmon River. If you reach the river, you have gone too far.

The logging road does not appear on topo maps for this area. Though

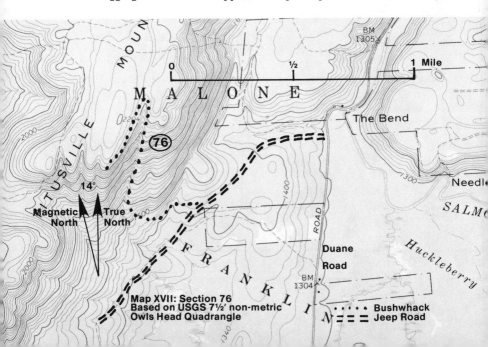

unpaved, it was in very good shape as of the fall of 1987. Drive or walk 0.7 mile along this road to the crest of a downgrade. At the bottom of the hill, a stream runs under the road from the west. There is a grassy place to park just below the top of the hill off the east shoulder.

Do not go down the hill any farther, but leave the road from this point, heading westerly, about 305° true north, heading into a mixed stand of young conifers under scattered large hardwoods. At 120 yards, you cross an intermittent stream that flows from the north.

At 135 yards, you come out of spruce growth and into pure hardwoods. So far, there has been little elevation gain, but at 155 yards, the slope begins to steepen with ledges ahead. Bear left and traverse upward under the ledges. At 290 yards, you pass through a zone that has been recently logged. This is state land, part of the Franklin State Forest, but since it is not part of the Forest Preserve, timber harvesting is allowed here.

You should arrive at a streambed running down from right to left at 335 yards. From here, follow a 300° true compass bearing on a gradient at first easy, then moderate, then steep to the crest of a hogback at 485 yards. Now, ahead of you and to the right, you should (especially if the leaves are down) be able to see a tremendous cliff—maybe 450 feet high and nearly perfectly vertical. Its top is your destination.

Turn right and follow the crest of the hogback a little farther and then bear left, skirting the edge of the cut-over area, to intercept the brook that flows along the base of the cliff at about 560 yards. Ignore any tributaries coming in from the right.

This is one of many beautiful little streams in the northern Adirondacks that were never named by the map makers. Phil Gallos calls it Boulderfall Brook for reasons that will soon be obvious.

Follow it upstream at moderate grades. At 795 yards, there is a 50° dogleg left in the stream's course. Climbing now becomes steep up a boulder fall. This is a very interesting feature of the mountain—a long, relatively narrow and deep strip of boulders ranging in size from hassocks to overstuffed chairs with a few sofas scattered about. The brook tumbles over and through the boulder fall, and climbing up along it is a visual treat. Just make sure you take care with your footing.

At 875 yards, the grade eases to moderately steep. It eases further, to moderate, at 930 yards. This is essentially the top end of the boulder fall. Continue following the brook. The grade becomes easy as you begin to enter a notch at 980 yards. This is another very picturesque part of the

From cliff on Titusville Mountain, view of Salmon River Valley and Lyon Mountain

mountain. The notch narrows considerably at 1105 yards, and you reach its upper portal at 1170 yards. From this point onward, the grade is very easy up to the source of Boulderfall Brook in a small, grassy swamp at a height-of-land at 1315 yards, 0.75 mile.

You do not have to walk all the way to the source, though. Anywhere you choose above the upper end of the notch would be fine to begin the last leg of the ascent. You need to nearly reverse direction, heading southwesterly so that you walk a course below the crest of the mountain and above the cliff top.

Approximately 0.25 mile will bring you to a small opening just above the highest part of the cliff. From this place, there is a superb view of the upper Salmon River Valley and surrounding heights from Owls Head Mountain (east-northeast) to St. Regis Mountain (southwest). Between those points, the panorama includes, from left to right, Ellenburg, Lyon, and Ragged Lake mountains; Norton Peak and the Haystacks; the Elbow and Plumadore Ranges; Esther and Whiteface (east-southeast), Baldface in front of the Loon Lake Mountains; a glimpse of Algonquin, Boundary, and Iroquois Peaks; with Debar Mountain dominating the view southward behind Studley Hill. You should allow at least an hour and a half to reach this point.

This is a good spot for a long break—perhaps lunch—before resuming your southwestward walk. In fairly short order, now, you come to a group of southwest facing ledges. From here, the vista extends from Lyon Mountain around to St. Regis and then, southwest to west-northwest, includes a startling, fascinating prospect of the southern ramparts of Titusville Mountain. It is easy to see now that what you have been climbing on is just a buttress of a much larger structure, and what you are looking at is only the south end of that structure. There is as much, if not more, to the north. Clearly, Titusville Mountain invites further exploration.

Immediately west of the ledges, there is a well-defined ravine that seems like a logical route back down to the logging road. In fact, it is; there is just one problem. Following the watercourse that flows out of the ravine, it is about 1240 yards down to the road, but a little less than halfway there, you cross onto cut-over land growing up so thickly with saplings that you can hardly see your feet, much less where you are going. That is the way it will be for the rest of your walk. The upper half of the route is quite interesting and sometimes very pretty. The lower half is just plain nasty. If you are looking for some real bushwhacking—where the bushes whack back—this is the way to go. Otherwise retrace your steps.

Northern Danglers

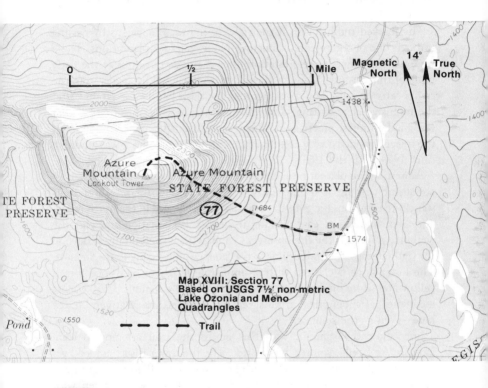

Map XVIII: Section 77
Based on USGS 7½' non-metric
Lake Ozonia and Meno
Quadrangles

▬ ▬ ▬ ▬ Trail

77 Azure Mountain Trail

Marked trail, unmanned fire tower
2 miles round trip, 2 hours, 1000-foot vertical rise, map XVIII

A relatively short climb takes you to the top of this outlying peak in a currently isolated tract of Forest Preserve. From the summit you view an expanse of northern Adirondack boreal forest and, on a clear day, some of the distant High Peaks.

The mountain is so remote it was not visited by Colvin until 1883. From its summit, he could see more than thirty of the signal stations of the Adirondack Survey; prominent among them Mount Marcy and

Whiteface, Algonquin, and Emmons (today Blue) mountains. Azure Mountain still seems to be in the middle of nowhere but the views are just as great. Drive 7 miles down Blue Mountain Road past its intersection with County Route 458; this intersection is approximately 4 miles south of St. Regis Falls.

The marked trailhead is on the right of the road; it begins by passing through one of the region's numerous Norway spruce plantations. These were early attempts at reforestation after the disastrous fires of the early years of this century. Many of these fires were caused by sparks from the trains carrying logs. The sparks ignited the slash left on the ground after the intensive clear-cutting so prevalent in the logging operations of that era. Modern forest practices are much more scientific and restrained, but the tower provided a very useful service during the decades it was manned, from 1914 until the 1970s.

Adjoining the plantation is a wetland with the showy yellow flowers of cowslips blooming in spring. Early settlers in the northern Adirondacks substituted cowslips for spinach, a custom still followed in the north today. After ten minutes of easy walking through the plantation and past the wetland, you reach the fire observer's cabin with its outbuildings. Beyond the outbuildings, the trail begins to rise steeply and steadily to the summit. The lower slope is clothed with an immature northern hardwood forest; yellow and white birch appear about midway to the summit. Unlike most medium-sized mountains in this region, conifers are relatively scarce here—even at the summit.

Just below the summit, waterbars across the trail attempt to stem erosion. At 1 mile, you reach the crest. The fire tower is surrounded by a grove of shadbush and chokecherry. The tower's lower flights of stairs have been removed to prevent climbing. All around is a sea of green with distant peaks in the far horizon to the south. The open rock face to the south of the summit stands out from down below as an almost perpendicular cliff. Ravens frequently soar overhead. The cliffs are the perfect site for falcons, and the state has used the cliff face of Azure as a hacking site to release young birds. Walk around the top for intimate glimpses of boreal forests with their wetlands and swamps—a vast sea of green through which winds the St. Regis River.

Iron, Charcoal, and Pulp

THE OUTLYING PEAKS and valleys that occupy the northeast quadrant of this guide have three things in common: iron, charcoal, and pulp.

Among the earliest iron works was the bloomery at Franklin Falls, begun in 1827. Isaac McLenathan and William Wells built a mill, forge, and small community there (it was originally called McLenathan Falls, and the name was changed in 1851). In 1852, the sawmill, houses, and stacks of lumber burned in a tremendous fire. The rebuilt mill survived until 1879. A fourteen-mile plank road was built from Black Brook to Franklin Falls in 1856.

In 1840 the manufacturing of iron in the northern counties brought more revenues, nearly half the total from all sources, than did lumbering. As late as 1880, the north country was producing fifteen percent of the nation's iron ore, mostly because of the unusual purity of the ores: they contained little or no sulfur or phosphorus.

J & J Rogers Company of Ausable Forks started producing iron in 1832. There were forges along Black Brook and at the Forks, and mines on Arnold and Palmer hills. In 1860 the company made 6000 tons of iron and 55,000 kegs of nails using 1,600,000 bushels of charcoal. By 1870 their forges consumed 4,500,000 bushels of charcoal a year. At its height, the company employed over 2000 men, 500 of them to cut, haul, and burn wood to produce charcoal in fifty kilns. The four Rogers' forges with twenty-two fires consumed the wood on 1000 acres a year. While the mines and forges lie generally to the east of this guide, the hills to the west supplied most of the charcoal.

The company owned most of Whiteface Mountain and began harvesting hardwoods there for charcoal in 1860. A settlement of French Canadians in the valley between Whiteface and the Stephenson Range was known as Little Montreal. Its men walked long miles to harvest lumber, an average of two cords a day, worth $.65 a cord, though sometimes as little as $.50. It took 2¼ cords of wood to produce 100 bushels of charcoal, worth $.06 each, but 300 to 500 bushels of charcoal were needed to make a ton of iron.

The company had three groups of kilns, two on the roads between Black Brook and Franklin Falls, north of the Stephenson Range. Eventually, a narrow gauge railway was built from near Little Montreal to the kilns. The Upper or West Kilns were at the LaHart farm at the foot of Catamount, section 92. Middle Kilns were located two miles to the east, while the Lower Kilns were just northeast of Summit House near the intersection of Silver Lake and Forestdale roads.

In the 1880s as the iron era was drawing to a close, J & J Rogers Co. owned over a hundred thousand acres of woodlands. In 1892 the company stopped all iron production, closing all its mines and forges. In 1893 the company began harvesting softwoods from the slopes of Whiteface for pulp. That year a pulp mill and dam were constructed on the West Branch of the Ausable. Later, a 2.5-mile-long flume was built below High Falls Gorge to bring the 4-foot spruce and balsam logs to the mill.

Early on, there were objections to the clear-cutting and pollution caused by these activities. The Plattsburgh *Sentinel* editorialized that "the one lamentable feature of the enterprise is the fact that soon the old growth sentinels that adorn and embellish the mountain (Whiteface), will give way to an exposure of rock, ledge, and cliff, and will stand out in the cold dull outline against the Adirondack sky—the rugged, nude relic of a once beautiful thing of nature."

Today this sentinel bears even more scars, making it the most easily identified point of reference in this corner of the Adirondacks.

Whiteface

Whiteface is one of the most unusual mountain groups in the Adirondack region. This massif sits isolated and alone north of the principal High Peaks region. Both Whiteface and its sister slope, Esther, are numbered among the High Peaks that rise over 4000 feet. Whiteface's summit, at 4867 feet towers above Lake Placid, elevation 1858 feet. Its face, carved by ski trails and slides, is the sentinel beacon for the northern Adirondacks. Some climbers disparage the mountain because of its nordic ski trails, roads, the buildings of the Atmospheric Sciences Research Center, which sit at the site of the old ski lodge below Marble Mountain, and the research silo on the summit.

Its lower slopes were cleared by settlers; the upper slopes were logged and logged heavily for the hardwoods that were taken for charcoal. Fires have ravaged some of its slopes. The mountain has a long history of agriculture, forestry, and finally recreation.

Historically, culturally, and economically, this is the most diverse, yet specialized mountain in the state. The mountain's historical vignettes that tell of the societal roots of the northern Adirondacks compensate for the mountain's loss of wilderness.

With its history of forest clearing and recovering, there are more examples of forest return and more tree species here than on any other mountain in the Adirondacks. There is no old growth virgin timber, yet twenty species of trees populate its forests. Red oak and red pine grow on the lower slopes. In the abandoned agricultural lands, starting at about 1300 feet, there are stands of second growth hardwoods reaching maturity. Fragments of alpine meadow fill pockets in the rocky summit.

On Marble Mountain, above the ski tow, there is an old ski route to the top of the road loop at 4000 feet. From there on up, in sight and sound of the Whiteface Memorial highway from Wilmington, you have the Castle, a restaurant, a tunnel and elevator to the summit silo, and the clouds that almost always seem to swirl around this major peak.

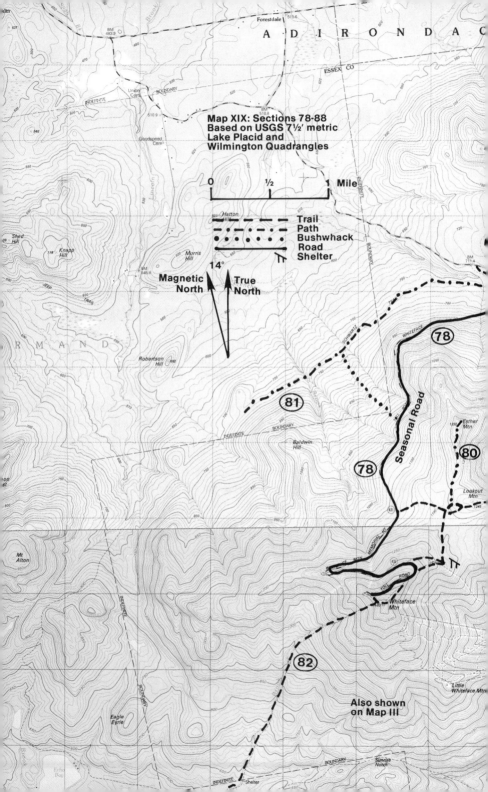

A D I R O N D A C

Forestdale

ESSEX CO

**Map XIX: Sections 78-88
Based on USGS 7½' metric
Lake Placid and
Wilmington Quadrangles**

0   ½   1 Mile

- - - - Trail
· · · · Path
- · - · Bushwhack
━━━━ Road
Shelter

**Magnetic
North**   14°   **True
North**

⑦⑧

⑧①

⑦⑧

⑧⓪

⑧②

**Also shown
on Map III**

78 Whiteface Memorial Highway
Road, hiking, cross-country skiing, map XIX

From Wilmington it is a short 3 miles west along an old highway to a "Y" where the left turn takes you to Whiteface Memorial Highway, the 5-mile toll road constructed in the 1930s. A $4 fee is charged per vehicle from mid-May through mid-October when the highway is open. Hikers and winter skiers traverse the road for free, but there is no vehicle parking near the toll house by Lake Stevens, so park near the "Y."

Scientists reach the research facilities on the mountain via snowmobiles in winter, leaving packed trails that invite cross-country skiers. The first 1.5 miles is a windswept straight stretch that can be brutally cold in winter. Picnic tables at 1.2 miles offer views north and a vista of dying spruce above. The first big turn at 2877 feet has a dramatic view west.

In the next 2 miles there is a series of sweeping turns. At 2 miles you pass a rocky bank and ravine, the site of the Atmospheric Science Research Center's test sites; you are below Esther at this point. As you approach the 3307-foot level (elevation signs are located at key points), you have a first view of the summit with its silo and dome facility. The 4000-foot level has the nicest stopping place with picnic tables at a turn. Notice how dwarfed the trees have become. A half mile farther up you are directly west of Lookout Mountain, the highest point of the old Marble Mountain Ski Area. Another half mile takes you to a dramatic landslide, the result of an avalanche two decades ago.

In the last 1.5 miles of highway, there are two hairpin turns. From the first you look directly down onto Lake Placid. In the next two-thirds mile, there is a panorama toward Wilmington with views from northwest to northeast. From the Wilmington turn, you look down on the ski center and across Wilmington Notch to Lake Champlain. Another half mile brings you to the parking area where you can hike up to the castle and take the 0.2 mile nature trail to the summit, though this is precarious in all but dry weather. In summer you can take the elevator to the top, 26 stories up. Either way, you have a spectacular view of the High Peaks to the south.

In winter, your ski down from the parking area takes but a fraction of the time it took you to ascend, so pay careful attention to conditions. The grade is such that you will go quite fast and it is easy to take a fall either on ice or in drifts of soft snow.

79 Whiteface from Wilmington

Hiking, camping
5.2 miles, 3 hours, 3620-foot ascent, map XIX

The beginning of the trail up Whiteface can be confusing. Drive up the Memorial Highway for 0.6 mile to a sign saying "Reservoir Road" and a DEC sign that indicates a red trail (its distance and elevation information are incorrect). Turn left up the road for 0.25 mile to the Wilmington Waterworks. You can park, but do not stray from the trail as you will be trespassing as the signs clearly warn. Cross the bridge on the outlet of the reservoir almost between no trespassing signs. Across the bridge, turn immediately right, as straight goes to posted lands.

As you enter the woods you find a forest of white cedars, hemlocks and paper birch. On your right, oblique to the trail, is an old stone fence. The canopy consists of red and white pine. The first 0.5 mile is fairly straight, then you angle left on a long and monotonous traverse of the east side of Marble Mountain. As the trail begins to rise, white pine and American beech are the more common forest types. After you cross a second stream, the cover changes; eastern hop hornbeam and white ash are mixed with mature red oak. There are lots of fallen old aspen trees and a few conifer seedlings.

At 1.5 miles, the trail suddenly becomes quite steep. You are ascending the ridge of Marble Mountain, which is 0.5 mile away, at a sharp angle. Here you encounter a fourth forest type, with pine, paper birch, quaking aspen, and stands of red pine that are unusual.

Along the ridgeline, near the subsummit of Marble Mountain, there is an abrupt end to the steep portion of the trail. Here in a flat portion of the trail, the trail makes a right angled turn right, then another to the left. At the right turn, there is a short trail to the top of Marble Mountain that leads to facilities of the Atmospheric Science Research Center. Hikers are discouraged from following this as there are no DEC trails in the vicinity and no public parking in the area.

Instead, turn left and continue up along the ridge, which is now open with good views. In the next quarter mile you can look out toward Esther and Big Basin, and down to the North Pole Resort with the Stephenson Range beyond. Smooth mountain alder covers this windswept portion of the ridge. Then, at about 2.6 miles, you turn into the woods and continue on the ridgeline for the next mile, going up and down through spruce and balsam fir forests. The way is mostly up, however, but levels off as you approach Lookout Mountain. At 3.5 miles, on the top of the ridgeline, you see the old toboggan shelter. It is near a hairpin turn on the highway where several decades ago there was a ski trail complex. It had rope tows, trails, and a lodge of which only the fireplace still stands.

Continue along the top, flat portion of the ridgeline to a shelter, at 4.5 miles. It is just below the Wilmington turn on the highway and in poor repair. Nevertheless, it is a good spot for lunch, with views toward Esther. The route is gentle for another fifteen minutes to the Wilmington turn. Suddenly there is a giant wall of rotten masonry ahead. Walk up to its base and follow paint blazes along it to the edge of the highway. The road is to the right. Scramble over a rocky ledge at the end of the rock work. Here the trail leaves the road again and heads into low spruce trees to the left along a ridge. Trees are now much smaller; there are two or three bluffs with outlooks before the transition from dwarf trees to the open summit.

You will see such alpine plants as alpine bilberry and crowberry, club mosses, and sandworts near the summit. You look out from the trail to the highest of the mountain's lifts, and a few minutes later reach the buildings at the top. Pause to enjoy the lovely views of the High Peaks to the south. From here you can retrace your steps or walk down the highway. A through trip, descending via Connery Pond, section 82, is a very long day's adventure.

80 Esther

Unmarked path, but not a bushwhack, map XIX

An unmarked path leads from the Whiteface Trail, section 79, to the 4240-foot summit of Esther. The point the path leaves the trail is not well marked. If you are coming up from Marble Mountain, in the level area near the toboggan shelter, you pass a couple turnouts to Lookout Mountain, which is just 100 yards off the upland side of the trail. One of these paths is marked by a pile of rocks on a slab on a small rise. A second starts opposite an old white sign directing the hiker back toward Marble Mountain. Both lead to Lookout Mountain, as they join after a few minutes. The combined path quickly rises to a small plateau, marked by a large, head-high rock at the right side of the trail. Behind the rock and partially out of sight is the decaying foundation of the old ski lodge, the center of a complex of ski trails that formerly crisscrossed these slopes between Whiteface and Esther. Continue past this height-of-land; the path dips briefly to the southwest (enough to make you think you are headed in the wrong direction) but then swings right, northerly, across the saddle toward Esther, a short 0.5 mile farther. The path along the ridgeline may be difficult to follow as balsam branches are growing over the trail, hiding the foot tread. Watch your feet to reassure yourself that you stay on the path. This would be impossible in winter.

Ten minutes past the lodge site there is a rise from which you can look back to Lookout, 0.25 mile away and about level with the rise. You head back into the woods again, and in less than fifteen minutes, you reach the summit—a high point where the path ends. A Forty-sixer canister marks the spot, as does a rock plaque to Esther McComb who inadvertently climbed this peak, while intending to head to Whiteface.

Vigorous growth of balsam has changed significantly the cover in the past twenty years, but the route is still a clear path. It should take no more than an hour up and back from the Whiteface Trail to visit Esther's summit. The only real problem, at the rock, won't get you lost, it just might make you miss a lookout.

81 Schwarz Trail
Unmarked path along an old road, map XIX

In the mountainous heap that is Whiteface, it is absolutely amazing to find a long, level, and relatively straight route such as this along an old road on the west side of Whiteface. The road headed from Little Montreal toward Lake Placid, and although it is filling in with trees, you can still follow it for nearly 3 miles. To reach the beginning, drive 0.7 mile west from the turnout to Whiteface, to a point near elevation 2334 feet at the beginning of the old road on the south.

The beginning is a bit confusing, since the path traverses a wet drainage, crossing a couple small streams, in an area where the path seems more densely filled with new saplings than its surroundings. Within five minutes you reach a dry road that follows a shelf with tall deciduous trees upslope, and evergreens downslope. The road seems to head straight as a die, even through a dry wash. It crosses a big dry gully, a second deep gully, then dips in a big curve to approach a stream from a bank fifteen feet above it. The stream is 1.7 miles from the road, nearly an hour's walk. Across the stream blue blazes mark an old route uphill, but they no longer lead anywhere.

The road, still dry on the shelf below the ridge, was obviously a dug road.

In twenty minutes, at 2.15 miles, you cross another Frenchs Brook, with small waterfalls both up and downstream. A pathway up the west bank leads again to the roadway, now densely overgrown but still obvious. The forest has changed; the trees are much taller. Finally, in a draw at 2.8 miles between the mountain and a small knob to the north, the road, still heading southwest, all but disappears, although even here you believe you can still follow it.

If you want an unusual trip, you can bushwhack uphill, either from the blue blazes headed south southeast, or from a point halfway between the streams, headed southeast. Either route will take you to the Memorial Highway, along which you can quickly head downhill to return to your car. You will not get lost on the bushwhack as the major streams on either side of the route will keep you from straying on your route uphill to the highway.

82 Whiteface Mountain from the South

Hiking, camping
6.6 miles, 4 hours, 3232-foot vertical climb, maps III and XIX

The first 3 miles of this trail are along the logging road to Whiteface Landing. (An interesting alternate beginning would be to paddle north the length of Lake Placid to the landing in the far northeast corner.) At the intersection of the Landing Trail and the Connery Pond Trail, turn right on the red trail, and head east for another mile, the levelest part of the trip so far. The trail crosses and recrosses Whiteface Brook three times. Just before the lean-to there is an open field, an old skid yard, above which Whiteface towers majestically.

A stream flowing from Sunrise Notch joins Whiteface Brook near the lean-to. The lean-to is a few minutes walk past the clearing, and it sits on high ground in a state of disrepair. Beyond the lean-to, the trail begins to climb; the next half hour is a pleasant climb along a moderate grade high on the right bank above Whiteface Brook. Spruce and yellow birch indicate there was no serious logging here.

At about 5 miles, the trail heads east away from the stream, briefly following a contour; this is the last time you will not be out of breath. The way becomes steeper and more challenging, and the last 1.5 miles is

View north from Whiteface to the Stephenson Range

straight up the south slopes with no breaks. Balsam fir and paper birch line the upper slopes. You can see the east arm of Lake Placid through the trees in the fall. As you continue up, you are directly opposite from Little Whiteface, which lies a mile off to your right, east. This distinctive feature of the skyline is the shoulder of Whiteface where chair lifts bring skiers in the winter.

The balsam fir grow smaller, and the canopy comes down to greet you. At one point, a log ladder aids your climb. Suddenly you see the top of Whiteface, a big table rock, an impressive, looming grey rock rising steeply over the sea of balsams like a giant wave. Trees give way to rock as you cross the timberline and follow orange blazes over rocks as the trail meanders to the top. It takes an hour and a half of hard work to climb from the lean-to to the openness of the alpine zone. The trail ends abruptly on the flat summit ridge in the midst of summertime tourists who have come this way by car.

This is an unusual route in that it begins and ends in a tourist environment, with a lovely stretch of wild lands in between and a really challenging climb at the end. You can either have a car spotted here at the summit of Whiteface, or walk the 5 miles down the highway toward Wilmington.

83 High Falls Gorge
Short trails, map XIX

A commercial venture owns one of the most attractive spots along the Ausable River east of Whiteface. There are maintained trails, bridges, and a restaurant at High Falls Gorge, all for a modest entrance fee. It is open only from Memorial Day weekend to Columbus Day.

A stand of old-growth forest lines the river here. The river tumbles over a series of three waterfalls, plunging 700 feet through a deep, walled gorge. Potholes carved by rushing glacial meltwater are found along the river bed, some high on the walls, way above the level of the river today. One is said to be the largest in the Adirondacks. The walls are formed of anorthosite, a pinkish granite, and black bands of basalt.

Graded trails, some with no stairs to climb, lead you along a marked network of short trails. A map and brochure with more of the natural history of the gorge goes with the ticket of admission.

Stephenson and Wilmington Ranges

84   Cooperkiln Pond

Trail, hiking, snowshoeing
2.7 miles, 1½ hours, 870-foot elevation change, map XIX

While the recent USGS metric maps call it Cooper Kill, most local signs and local usage spell it Cooperkiln. From the main four corners of Wilmington, head west on NY 431 toward Whiteface. At 1.6 miles you pass Santa's North Pole Theme Park on your right. To orient yourself for this and other trips in the Stephenson Range, look north from the park's parking area on the south side of the road. To the north, the cliffs of Winch Mountain appear to the right, east of the park. Morgan Mountain is on the skyline behind and to the left, west, of Winch. Cooperkiln Pond lies out of sight, behind and to the east of Morgan Mountain.

Continue west on NY 431 and bear right at 2.9 miles on the Bloomingdale-Franklin Falls Road, passing the beginning of Whiteface Memorial Highway and Lake Stevens. At 3.6 miles there is a trailhead sign on the right, north, pointing to Cooperkiln Pond, 2.7 miles. The trail is marked with red DEC markers and begins on an old tote road, starting at an elevation of 2360 feet (720 meters). Head northeast for 100 yards to a "T" intersection and turn left to follow the red markers west on a second tote road. Shortly take the right and more traveled fork. In a few minutes this route swings east into a clearing and becomes more of a trail than a tote road.

The trail, still with adequate red markers, swings southeast, fairly level, and crosses a wet stretch and a small brook. After twenty minutes, the trail turns north and climbs gently in a balsam, yellow and white birch, and striped maple forest. Surely these are signs this was once burned. The trail, again on a section of old tote road, begins to climb and follow a small brook, which is to the right of the trail. The trail is somewhat eroded and wet as it heads northeast. After fifty minutes, at 1.2 miles, you cross a pair of brooks on two log bridges, both brooks flowing to your left. The climb continues fairly steadily.

After an hour and ten minutes, at 1.7 miles the trail is still climbing steadily, now more to the east with the headwaters of Frenchs Brook flowing westward in a steep valley to your left, north. Yellow birch and spruce dominate the forest as the trail levels in a meadow at the head of Frenchs Brook. After an hour and twenty minutes of hiking, just short of 2 miles, the trail reaches the height-of-land at 3230 feet (988 meters) north of Morgan Mountain and begins a gradual descent to Cooperkiln Pond.

Whiteface from Morgan Mountain

During the winter, the small pass catches large quantities of snow that create a winter wonderland of heavily bowed spruce trees.

The trail follows a small drainage, then crosses it, and continues along with the drainage now to the right of the trail. Shortly, you can see the pond through the trees. Cross the inlet on logs and then the outlet, again on logs, before reaching the Cooperkiln Pond Lean-to. The shallow pond lies at 3010 feet, 918 meters, and is studded with a variety of photogenic glacial erratics. The unnamed 1026-meter peak Wilmington Range forms a backdrop to the northeast of the pond.

Section 87 describes a northern approach to the pond, which is the preferred cross-country ski approach. You can return to your car in under an hour, or continue on using section 87, if you have spotted a car at Bonnieview Avenue as that section describes.

85 Morgan Mountain

Bushwhack, map XIX

The bushwhack begins from the col on the north side of Morgan Mountain at the height-of-land on the Cooperkiln Pond Trail. Elevation here is 3230 feet (985 meters). Leave the trail here and bushwhack due south through a level section of moderately thick spruce. The route then climbs gently to reach the summit ridge of Morgan Mountain. A short distance east of the actual summit, there is a fairly recent slide on the eastern, false summit of Morgan, where birch trees have slid away to expose bare rock. If you are careful, you can get an unobstructed view to the southeast from this slide, so you look directly down on the hamlet of Wilmington.

After a total bushwhack of about twenty-five minutes, you reach the main summit of Morgan (3460 feet, 1054 meters). It provides only a few screened views of Whiteface Mountain through spruce, balsam, and dead trees. To return to the main trail, return first to the false summit and head due north for about fifteen minutes.

86 Two Unnamed Summits of the Stephenson Range

Bushwhacks, map XIX

From the Cooperkiln Pond Lean-to, head west along the red-marked trail and cross the pond's outlet and inlet. About 100 yards west of the pond, leave the trail and bushwhack on a bearing of 160° true, 175° magnetic. Almost immediately, the route begins to climb moderately through white birch, spruce, and balsam. It takes but twenty minutes to reach the 3326-foot (1014-meter) summit. Through the trees there are peek-a-boo views from left to right through the south of Whiteface, Iroquois, Algonquin, Avalanche, Colden, the Sentinel Range with Marcy behind Morgan, and Catamount.

To the east of true north, 5°, you see the 1054-meter summit of the Wilmington Range, section 88. The summit you are on actually consists of two peaks, separated by a low north to south depression. The western knob provides the better views.

From the eastern summit knob, head toward the 962-meter peak on a bearing of 70°. It takes only fifteen minutes to get to the broad flat col that separates it from the first summit. Hunters use this col as a base camp for hunting. Another thirty minutes of hiking, with only moderate climbing, and you reach the 3155-foot (962-meter) summit.

The south side of this second summit consists of broad bare rock ledges. The ledges afford a truly superb and unobstructed view from 220° around to the south-southeast, east, and northeast to 45°. This may be the most worthwhile vista in the Stephenson Range. You can see Taylor Pond, Lake Champlain and Malletts Bay (at 50°), Trembleau Mountain, Poka-moonshine Mountain, Camels Hump, Hamblin Mountain, Arnold Mountain, the Jay Range with Slip and Saddleback mountains behind, Giant, the Sentinel Range with Mount Marcy behind, Algonquin, Indian Pass, and Whiteface Mountain. It is a very special place. Be sure to allow adequate time to enjoy this view.

From this second summit you can return to Cooperkiln Pond Lean-to by heading west at 270° true. Cross the col between the two summits on this bearing and after crossing the col, turn on to a bearing of 300°, 315° magnetic, and contour around the northeast side of the higher, 3326-foot, first summit through white birch and bramble. Allow an hour and fifteen minutes to return to the main red-marked trail that leads to the Cooperkiln Pond Lean-to.

Those who wish to enjoy the special views of the lower summit without climbing the taller one, should start at the same point, 100 yards west of the lean-to, on a bushwhack bearing of 120°, 135° magnetic, to the col and then head 105° magnetic to the summit. Allow an hour and a half to reach it and at least three hours for the round trip, from the trail.

87 Cooperkiln Pond via Pettigrew Brook

Trail, hiking, skiing
2.9 miles, 2 hours, 1684-foot vertical rise, map XIX

From the main four corners of Wilmington, head northeast on Bonnieview Avenue, County Route 19A. At 0.9 mile, bear left, staying on Bonnieview as Preston Road veers to the right. At 3.2 miles, you reach the intersection with John Bliss Road on the right. On the left, west at this intersection is a sign marking the trail to Cooperkiln Pond Lean-to 3.6 miles, which is incorrect. There is room to park along the road. The starting elevation is 1320 feet (403 meters).

The trail begins on a tote road, marked with red DEC markers. You head northwest at 225° magnetic through an impressive forest of tall white pine. The road turns west and the number of white birches increases. Cross a brook flowing to your left. After fifteen minutes the road begins to climb slightly.

The road, continuing to climb westward, follows an esker-like ridge that drops off on one side to a tributary of Big Brown Brook and on the other side to Pettigrew Brook. To the south you can hear the latter brook, and through the trees you can see the flanks of the 3155-foot, 962-meter summit described in section 86.

After about a half hour, 1.2 miles, you reach a fork in the road at elevation 1820 feet (555 meters). Follow the red markers to the right on the more traveled and more level route. The left fork leads to Pettigrew Brook and a potential camping spot.

Past the fork, the tote road turns northwest and climbs more steeply. It becomes more rocky. At an elevation of 2180 feet, 665 meters, the route turns sharply to the left. This elbow can clearly be seen on the metric map. The junction here at 1.7 miles is reached about 50 minutes from the start of the trip. The tote road straight ahead to the northwest goes a short distance before it ends at another possible camping spot, not far from the upper reaches of a tributary of Big Brown Brook. Snowmobile trail signs also mark this elbow in the tote road.

After turning left onto the trail, you head 215° true, 230° magnetic on the level, or slightly dropping section through a white birch and striped maple forest. You cross several drainages until you cross one that is prominent enough to cause a jog in the trail. This is Pettigrew Brook and soon you recross to its left bank and climb in a spruce and yellow birch forest. The trail steepens, becomes more rocky, and crosses Pettigrew Brook again.

After twisting back and forth through a less distinct section, it crosses back to the left bank of the brook, which has now become much smaller. After less than two hours of hiking the trail levels off in a balsam forest and at 2.9 miles reaches the lean-to at Cooperkiln Pond. The pond can also be reached from the Bloomingdale-Franklin Falls Road, section 84. This approach has the most suitable grades for cross-country skiing, and after checking the trails from both directions, it can be recommended that a northwest to southeast through trip is realistic for expert skiers.

The return trip to Bonnieview Avenue will take about an hour and twenty minutes.

88   Two More Unnamed Peaks in the Wilmington Range

Bushwhacks, map XIX

Two unnamed peaks in the Wilmington Range north of Cooperkiln Pond, with elevations of 1026 and 1054 meters, offer good bushwhack destinations from the trail to that pond. Go west from the lean-to and cross the outlet and the inlet of the pond. Just west of the inlet leave the red-marked trail and bushwhack north along the west side of the pond, staying back from it. At the northeast corner of the pond, when you can sight the lean-to across the pond to the southeast on a bearing of 140° true, 155° magnetic, leave the pond and head due north for eight minutes to a ridge. Turn right to a bearing of 45° magnetic and bushwhack through a spruce thicket, skirting slightly east to avoid the worst sections. After twenty minutes of bushwhacking, generally on this 45° bearing, in spruce with some blowdown, you reach the 3365-foot, 1026-meter summit.

As you climb you can see the 1014-meter peak and Morgan Mountain of the Stephenson Range through the trees to the south, with Whiteface Mountain to the west of Morgan. The summit itself is covered in a mix of dead trees with some live birch. You have limited views of Union Falls Pond on the Saranac River to the northwest, 325° magnetic.

Leave this summit on a bearing of 50° magnetic heading for the slightly taller 3460-foot, 1054-meter summit that can be seen through the trees ahead. Ten minutes of hiking brings you to the col between the two summits, a drop of only about 30 feet. Another ten minutes of bushwhacking on a bearing of 20° brings you to the first of the two peaks of this summit. This first, and southernmost, peak has the best views. Actually the views begin before you reach the top and continue on top to provide a broken vista that extends from the northwest to the west and southwest. If you look carefully through the trees you can get good views of Whiteface and Esther and Catamount.

Another five minutes of hiking on the same bearing through a slight drop will bring you to the main peak of the 1054-meter summit, but this has no views. By continuing past the summit, you can see some interesting cliffs on the southeast side of another unnamed summit in the Wilmington Range.

The return trip to the pond takes forty-five minutes. Retrace your steps to the southern summit on a bearing of 215° true, 230° magnetic, and continue on the same bearing to the col and on to the lower summit. Continue down the ridge, still on the same bearing until you can see the pond to your left. Head south to the pond and follow its west shore around to the trail.

Duncan Mountain from Union Falls Road near Silver Lake Bog

Silver Lake and Taylor Pond

An odd patchwork of disconnected blocks of state land typifies the southern corner where Franklin and Clinton counties meet. Silver Lake and Taylor Pond lie in southwest Clinton County. They are similar in size, both trending southwest-northeast, just a mile apart. Both had resorts early on; the Rogers family (of the J & J Rogers Co.) had a camp at Silver Lake in the second half of the nineteenth century. Several acquisitions have brought the shores of Taylor Pond into the Forest Preserve, though most of the shores of Silver Lake remain privately owned.

The Nature Conservancy has a boardwalk trail through a swamp forest near Silver Lake. A snowmobile trail that is suitable for a long ski trek surrounds Taylor Pond. To the northeast of Silver Lake lies its namesake mountain, with a good trail and excellent views. To the northwest of the lake, north of Union Falls, lie Duncan Mountain and the Alder Brook Mountain Range, all with trailless peaks, good views, and challenging bushwhacks. To the south of Taylor Pond lies Catamount Mountain with one of the most delightful trails in the northern Adirondacks. Whether you want a long summer weekend of activities from a base at the nearby Taylor Pond Campground or a series of winter snowshoe and ski treks, you will find trails to suit in the tracts of Forest Preserve land that surround these bodies of water.

89 Silver Lake Camp Preserve
Nature trail, boardwalk, map XX

Silver Lake Camp offers a trail and boardwalk into a swamp forest in the midst of a fifty-two acre Nature Conservancy preserve. The boardwalk into the heart of the swamp forest is nearing completion, making it possible to visit an area that would ordinarily be too wet for exploration. Hummocks of sphagnum moss support a forest of balsam and red spruce that is taking over from hemlock and birch. White cedar and tamarack mingle with

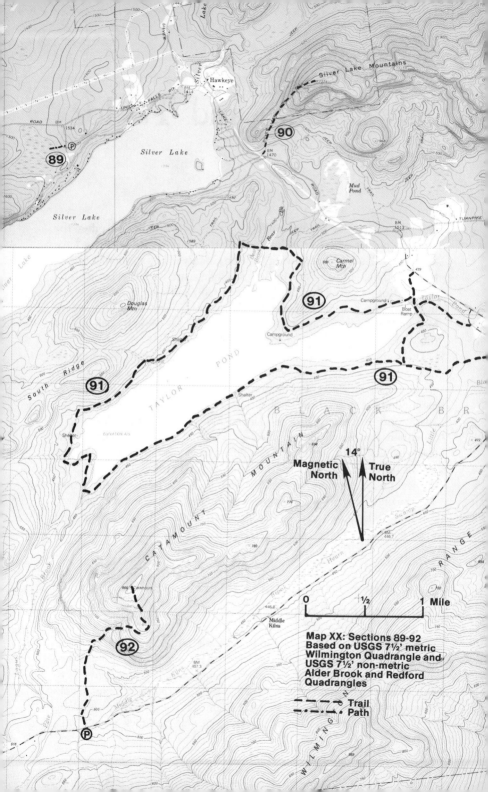

Map XX: Sections 89-92
Based on USGS 7½' metric
Wilmington Quadrangle and
USGS 7½' non-metric
Alder Brook and Redford
Quadrangles

14°

Magnetic North   True North

0   ½   1 Mile

Trail
Path

black spruce as the ground gets wetter. Gold thread, wood sorrel, creeping white winterberry or snowberry, lady slippers and trillium, and many ferns enjoy this typical swamp forest. The boardwalk leads to an opening in the forest cover—a typical bog with sheep laurel, labrador tea, leatherleaf, holly, and pitcher plants. Actually, there is a bog, with its sphagnum base that grades into a swamp with the heath shrubs. These two habitats overlap and grade into the surrounding swamp forest.

The preserve also includes higher ground that supports an impressive forest of hardwoods with mature trees standing like pillars in a cathedral sheltering a dark forest floor that supports little undergrowth. Black-backed woodpeckers forage for beetles in the black spruce in the bog. Pileated woodpeckers chop huge holes in the upland beech. The preserve rises to a ridge 400 feet above Silver Lake. The ridge is carpeted with the needles of red pine that grow on top of it.

To reach the preserve, drive west on Union Falls Road from its intersection with Silver Lake Road. Turn left 1 mile past the intersection and park on the right at 1.2 miles. A sign marks the entrance to the preserve.

Follow the trail west and after about 225 feet it becomes a boardwalk. There is a registration booth in another 150 feet. Beyond it, the boardwalk continues another 1200 feet through the preserve, with an extension to be completed in 1988.

90 Silver Lake Mountain

Hiking
0.9 mile, 40 minutes, 900-foot vertical rise, map XX

Silver Lake Mountain is a gem of a mountain with strikingly beautiful cliffs. Its wall of cliffs seems most imposing as you drive north from Black Brook toward Silver Lake. They are a traditional area for falcons to breed. There has been a trail on the mountain for years, but private land near the beginning of the trail has made its continued use questionable. Fortunately, the state has recently purchased access to the trail.

To find its beginning, go 1.8 miles north on Silver Lake Road from the entrance to Taylor Pond State Campground. The trail starts here on the east side of the road, just south of where the powerlines cross and directly opposite an access road to private camps on the south side of Silver Lake.

Starting at an elevation of 1470 feet, the trail heads northerly on an old tote road, level at first then gradually beginning to climb through a mixed deciduous forest. Painted red arrows on the rock and some very old trail markers help guide the way. The route is now a trail, climbing north partly on bare rock.

After fifteen minutes, you leave the bare rock and enter a pine forest with red DEC markers. You are climbing along a well-defined ridge, just northwest of its crest. The maturing pine, some over a foot in diameter, form a canopy over the trail. Steep sections and stands of balsam and white birch follow. At an elevation of 2040 feet, some boulders on the left provide a screened view of Alder Brook Mountain to the northwest.

From this point the trail begins to climb fairly steeply. At 2190 feet it skirts to the left of an open rock that provides an excellent unobstructed view down the axis of Silver Lake to the southwest. The trail has curved more northeast to 60° true and continues steeply up the open ridge or nose of the mountain. Views increase as you climb. Just before the summit, the trail enters the woods, then emerges on the summit at an elevation of 2374 feet. The climb takes about forty minutes.

The summit provides excellent views of Catamount Mountain, Taylor Pond, and Silver Lake. The near view of the granite gneiss cliffs of Silver Lake Mountain itself to the east and of Mud Pond in the foreground are especially nice. To the north, the view is obstructed by dense red pine, white spruce, and balsam that cover the north side of the summit.

91 Taylor Pond Loop

Hiking, cross-country skiing, camping
11 miles, 4½ hours, relatively level, map XX

A superb trail surrounds Taylor Pond, generally following old roads. The route can serve as a winter ski trek or a long summer hike. It leads past three lean-tos that are all accessible from the lake. Walking the loop, you enjoy lovely views of the lake and of Catamount Mountain.

To find the trailhead from the Northway, take NY 9N south from Exit 34 for 10.7 miles and turn right at the light in Ausable Forks. In one block, turn left on Black Brook Road (Fern Lake Road). At 11.7 miles bear left at a fork. At 13.8 miles turn left again toward Silver Lake and Black Brook. At 14.9 miles the road from Wilmington joins from the left; you stay straight for Silver Lake. At 20.2 miles there is a DEC sign on the left for the snowmobile trail at a dirt road leading left. This is also the entrance to the Taylor Pond Camping Area and a winter trek begins here at 0 mile.

Taylor Pond

The dirt road leads to the toll both in 0.4 mile and to the trailhead for the loop in 0.2 mile more. The sign says 14.2 miles for the loop, but it is really only 11 miles long.

Taylor Pond's campsites are very pretty, sheltered beneath pines, cedars, hemlocks, and birches. The trail begins through the campground heading gently uphill and slightly away from the lake. Routed along an old road, the trail is quite wide with gentle ups and downs and occasional wet spots.

After forty minutes, at 1.4 miles, you can see the water of Taylor Pond's northern bay straight ahead. The trail changes from the slightly south of west direction you have been following to a northerly course to round this bay. For a while you cannot see the shore, then you parallel it about 150 feet in. At 1.8 miles there is an unmarked fork right that leads to the tiny nub called Carmel Mountain. Stay straight and at 2.1 miles you reach another intersection where you turn left. Directional signs keep you on the proper route.

The trailside is handsome with many lichens, mosses, polypodies, and club mosses, and princess pine grow beneath the balsam, cedar, hemlock and white birch.

At 2.2 miles, about an hour from the start, the road you have been following goes straight ahead, but the trail takes a sharp left turn away from it to take a southwest heading. The place is marked. Nearby are the

trashy remains of an old logging camp. The trail leads briefly through a cedar swamp and then makes a very sharp right turn. A path straight leads to the shore of the bay near its inlet. A barely floating snowmobile bridge helps you across the inlet at 2.6 miles. Beyond the trail is a narrow path rather than an old road.

The trail winds uphill and the going is rough and bumpy. You pass an old clearing and turn south, following an old road again. You pass a tiny pond on the right, then climb, staying out of sight of Taylor Pond. You stay left at another junction. The next left at 3.8 miles leads to the north shore lean-to, but there is no sign to this effect. Many roadways fork left now, and the trail is very wet. You cross a small stream, and at 4.2 miles pass a spring bubbling out of the ground on your right, then the trail drops sharply toward the pond. Again you parallel the shore about 150 feet from it. The trail, again a narrow path, is rough going. A half hour from the spring, at about 5.2 miles, watch as you turn south at a point from which the pond is visible. The trail is behind, west of, the western lean-to at this point. The lean-to is clearly marked from the water but not from the shore, and there is no obvious path leading to it.

After bushwhacking back to the trail from the lean-to, you climb to a height-of-land, then drop to shore in a marshy inlet. Walk right for a short distance to find a beaver dam that you can use to cross the inlet stream. The trail goes straight across the water, in the fashion of snowmobile trails, so you will have to bushwhack back along the stream to find it again. There is heavy blowdown just after you regain the trail, and you must look sharp to stay on it. Keep right and head uphill. Past the blowdown, the trail, a narrow path, is level and fairly easy to follow.

The trail approaches a second bay, a shallow one with loons. Here, at 5.9 miles, crossing may not be difficult in low water, but in wet times, you will have to bushwhack upstream to look for a crossing. This may be quite a long detour. The path continues narrow, rough, and winding along the shore. There are more rocks and roots and ups and downs than on the other side of the pond. Finally, the trail intersects a roadway again, but shortly heads downhill in a very wet area, and crosses another brook at 7 miles. The trail continues very wet, crosses a small stream, but remains close to shore. At just short of 7.5 miles you have a hop-on-rocks crossing of a rushing brook and just across it there is the third lean-to. The setting is not as pretty as the lean-to on the north, but the lean-to is at least close to the trail.

Lean-to at Taylor Pond

Beyond the lean-to, the trail is a roadway that appears to be used by four-wheel-drive vehicles. It is badly rutted. Shortly you pass a magnificent stone chimney, all that remains of a former camp, except for a vast quantity of bottles, cans, and other debris. A path leads uphill, but the trail stays straight and very wet, passing through abandoned farmland. At 9.1 miles, forty minutes from the third lean-to, a roadway joins from the right (this leads to Forestdale Road, 0.5 mile south of its northern intersection with Silver Lake Road). You can use this to complete a loop, using the roads.

If you turn left, you will find the trail firms, but it is very far from the pond. A wide, well-used path leads left, down to the pond. You stay straight, out of sight of the pond, as the road becomes smooth. At 9.7 miles there is another junction. The way right parallels the outlet of Taylor Pond and leads to Forestdale Road near the bridge over the outlet and 0.1 mile south of Silver Lake Road.

If you turn left, you climb a steep knob and drop down to the earthen dam at the outlet of Taylor Pond. The trail leads past the boat ramp and up to the campground road. A right turn leads in 0.2 mile to your car at Forestdale Road, completing the loop.

92 Catamount from the South

Hiking
1.9 miles, 2 hours, 1568-foot vertical rise, map XX

Catamount is a huge mountain whose summit seems all the more imposing because there is so much open rock. The mountain was burned twice, once in the late 1870s and again in 1941. Half the time you are on the trail to the small bare cobble on its southern slopes and on to the summit, you walk on open rock, enjoying views all the way.

The trail to Catamount Mountain starts from Forestdale Road. The northeast end of Forestdale Road splits and joins Silver Lake Road at two places in the Town of Black Brook. The southern branch joins Silver Lake Road at East Kilns. From this point head northwest on Forestdale Road and bear left at 1 mile where the northern extension of Forestdale Road forks right.

Continue west and southwest on Forestdale Road. The Catamount Mountain range rises abruptly to your right, north, and the Wilmington Range is on your left. At 2.2 miles you reach a clearing that was once the

Catamount Summit from the Cobble

Middle Kilns. Here you have a good view of the cliffs of Catamount. At 4.7 miles two large red paint blazes on maple trees on the right side of the road mark the beginning of the trail. Just past this, the land along the road is marked with posted signs. This point is 0.7 mile east of where the Clinton-Franklin county line crosses Forestdale Road, just west of West Kilns.

The hike begins at an elevation of 1624 feet, 495 meters. The trail heads north in a mixed forest of balsam, maple, and yellow birch. In seven minutes, at 0.2 mile, you reach a stone cairn with a survey marker and posted signs marking the property to the west. A side trail leads into these posted lands.

Continue northwest as red paint blazes mark the posted land to the left. Cross a flat clearing that provides a view of Catamount to the northeast. After 20 minutes, at 0.7 mile, the trail descends slightly to cross a dry, sandy gully and then turns northeast. The forest becomes maple, beech, and white birch as you begin to climb moderately. At 1 mile (elevation 1870 feet, and about thirty minutes into the hike), the trail jogs sharply right. The trail is alternately steep and level. It crosses a stream, then climbs steeply at 2130 feet and heads northeast out of the stream valley. Occasional red DEC markers are visible; they are nailed on backwards as this is not a DEC trail.

The first bare rock view point is at 1.2 miles and 2490 feet elevation, about fifty minutes into the hike. Across the open rock, the trail is variously marked with cairns, white paint, and red DEC disks. The trail levels off over bare rock as you hike past the cliffs that form the cobble, elevation 2790 feet. The view from the base of the cobble looking up to the northeast is impressive, as is the panorama to the southwest. The trail dips briefly through a spruce forest and then climbs steeply out of the forest onto bare rock again.

The climb from the base of the cobble to its summit follows cairns and at one point is entrenched in a chimney formed by the erosion of a black mafic dike intrusion in the granitic gneiss that constitutes the bedrock of the mountain. Views south are unobstructed during this steep climb. An hour and twenty minutes into the hike, at 1.5 miles, you reach the summit of the cobble. You can see in all directions, although the looming main summit of Catamount fills the field of vision to the north.

From the cobble, the route follows cairns and white paint blazes across the exposed gneiss heading northerly. The trail dips into a shallow col with scrubby white spruce trees, then continues to climb steeply over bare rock to Catamount's summit. It takes about thirty minutes to hike the 0.4 mile from the cobble to the summit, for a total hiking time of a little under two hours from Forestdale Road.

The summit view is truly spectacular and is only obstructed by the ridge of Catamount itself as it heads off on a bearing of 20°. You can see Silver Lake Mountain, Taylor Pond, Silver Lake, Union Falls Pond, Duncan Mountain and the Alder Brook Range, Whiteface and Esther, and the Stephenson and Wilmington ranges. Two benchmarks, Catamount No. 1 and No. 2, both dated 1942, mark the 3168-foot, 966-meter, summit.

As you leave the summit note the cairns initially head off on a bearing of 100° true and gradually bend to the right as you descend to the cobble on a bearing of 170° true. The hike back to Forestdale Road takes about an hour and a quarter.

93 Duncan and Alder Brook Mountains
Bushwhack, map XXI

The Alder Brook Mountain Range is a wild and little used part of the Forest Preserve that straddles the Clinton and Franklin county line just south of NY 3. This trip begins at the corner of NY 3 and Silver Lake Road (Clinton County 13) in Clayburg. Go south on Silver Lake Road, over the

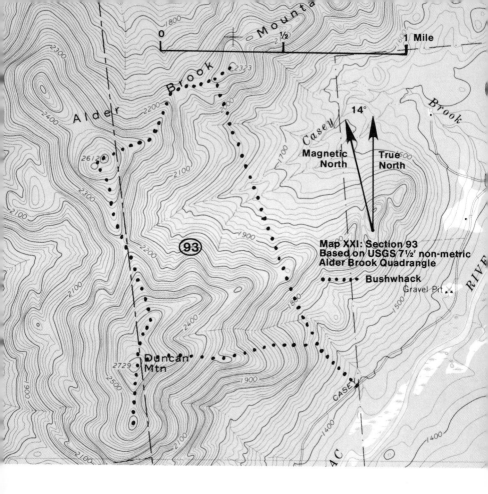

Map XXI: Section 93
Based on USGS 7½' non-metric
Alder Brook Quadrangle

•••••• Bushwhack

Saranac River at 3.9 miles, and turn right, west, on Union Falls Road at 5.8 miles in the Hamlet of Hawkeye. Follow Union Falls Road, County Route 17, west, crossing the Saranac River again, at 8.6 miles, just below the dam, and immediately turn right on Casey Road. Follow Casey Road as it forks left at 0.1 mile and park along it 1.2 miles from the Union Falls Dam where there is a red paint blaze on the left, northwest, marking the boundary of Forest Preserve land on the west, private land to the east.

You begin the bushwhack at an elevation of 1400 feet and head northwest at 315° true, 330° magnetic. You climb gently, then more moderately in a sugar maple forest. To your left there is a steep slope, but by continuing on the 330° bearing for fifteen minutes you avoid it. After fifteen minutes, at about 1720 feet elevation, turn left and take a new bearing of 265° magnetic. Keep the steep slope to your left as you continue the moderate climb.

View of Silver Lake Mountain from Duncan Mountain

After forty-five minutes, at an elevation of 2120 feet, you reach a bare rock prominence, which clearly shows as a blip on the topographic map. This is an excellent resting spot with views that stretch from 95° in the east through the south to 230° in the southwest. From here you can see Silver Lake Mountain, Silver Lake, Catamount Mountain, and Union Falls Pond with Whiteface Mountain behind.

From the rocky prominence continue west at 270° true, 285° magnetic, following the cliffs as far as you can. After reentering the woods, climb toward the summit of Duncan Mountain, skirting a spruce thicket by going around it to the right. About two hours from the start of your hike, about 1.3 miles, you reach a small clearing at the summit of Duncan Mountain, elevation 2729 feet. Views are screened by trees, though McKillip Mountain is clearly visible in the southwest.

If you go south from the highest point along the ridge, pushing through scrubby spruce for less than fifteen minutes, you come to a large open rock slope. The rock slants to the top of the cliffs that are visible from the south. From the open patch, there are great views south to Union Falls Pond and Silver Lake.

If you return to the summit and head back to the start along the same route, the return trip to Casey Road takes an hour following a bearing of 105° magnetic to the rocky viewpoint and then 100° to elevation 1700 feet where you turn right to a bearing of 150° to reach Casey Road.

To bushwhack over to Alder Brook Mountains, leave the summit of Duncan on a bearing of 15° true, 30° magnetic. After passing through a shallow col at an elevation of 2650 feet and after twenty minutes, turn left to a bearing of 355° magnetic. You can see Alder Brook Mountains through the trees. Stay on the ridge between Duncan and the 2612-foot summit of Alder Brook Mountains. The route is difficult at first through spruce and some blowdown and over moss covered ledges. After the initial difficulty, the forest opens up and you reach the col between Alder Brook Mountain and Duncan at an elevation of 2270 feet, about forty minutes from Duncan's summit.

The bushwhack up Alder Brook Mountain is through open maple forest. Continue on 355° magnetic, and an hour from Duncan, at 2480 feet elevation, if you look back, you have a good view of Duncan Mountain and Silver Lake to the right. An hour and a half and less than a mile from Duncan, you reach the southeastern portion of the twin summits at 2600-feet elevation. Continue northeast on a bearing of 70° magnetic for a short distance to reach the 2612-foot summit. There are no views from this highest point. But, continue on a bearing of 85° magnetic for about fifteen minutes through open forest until the slope steepens on the right. Then turn left to 45° magnetic and hike down to the col between the 2621-foot and the 2323-foot summits. You reach this col, elevation 2130 feet, after a descent of thirty minutes from the summit.

From the col continue northeast on a bearing of 70° magnetic and ten minutes of hiking brings you to the base, at 2240 feet, of a set of cliffs that form the ridge up to the 2323-foot summit. It takes only ten minutes from here to climb to the top of the cliffs, which provide unobstructed views of Duncan Mountain and the highest summit of Alder Brook Mountains to the southwest. Since the summit of the 2323-foot peak has no views, return to the base of the cliffs on a bearing of about 250° magnetic, less than ten minutes. From here you can complete the circuit by returning to Casey Road on a bearing of 155° magnetic, for a 1.5-mile bushwhack of just over an hour. This return crosses three intermittent branches of Casey Brook and a ridge that extends eastward from Duncan Mountain. You cross the first after ten minutes, the second in ten minutes more, and the third shortly after that. You cross the ridge at an elevation of about 2040 feet, thirty-five minutes from the base of the cliffs. The south side of this ridge has small cliffs that must be negotiated with care.

Continue on a bearing of 155° and you reach Casey Road in another half hour. The entire loop including Duncan and the two summits of Alder Brook Mountains will take about four hours.

Dannemora and Ellenburg

Two isolated patches of Forest Preserve cover parts of Ellenburg and Dannemora mountains in the far northeast corner of the park. Iron explains the growth of the nearby community of Dannemora. The Averill Mine was opened in 1842, the Fairbanks mine in 1861. Oddly enough, the Clinton State Prison at Dannemora was located there because of the iron and not because of its isolation. The first prison was built in 1845 by prisoners who were brought to the area to work in the iron mines and run the Catalan Forge built to process the ore. But, production did not live up to the expectations of the legislature, which had authorized the building of the prison in order to produce iron. The supply dwindled and production ceased shortly after 1852, but to this day there is a state prison at Dannemora. And now the Clinton Correctional Facility is the largest single employer in Clinton County.

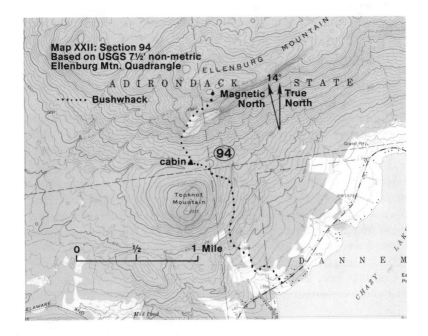

Map XXII: Section 94
Based on USGS 7½' non-metric
Ellenburg Mtn. Quadrangle

94   Ellenburg Mountain
Bushwhack, map XXII

The view north from Chazy Lake is dominated by Ellenburg Mountain, a significant trailless area of Forest Preserve land. Unfortunately, the exact boundaries between state and private lands in this area have been disputed for many years so some ingenuity is required to climb the mountain without trespassing.

The Ellenburg Mountain 7.5-minute Quadrangle shows a southern extension of Forest Preserve land that crosses NY 374 just north of Seine Bay on Chazy Lake. However, land along the highway here is considered private and is built up with private homes. So, the route to Ellenburg Mountain begins just east of the southern extension of Forest Preserve land. To find the spot, head east along NY 374 from Chazy Lake Road. There is a gas station on the left, north, at 0.8 mile. Park just east of it at 0.9 mile at the top of a slight rise.

The route begins as a bushwhack by crossing a section of overgrown farmland on a bearing of 335° true. After bushwhacking through scrubby growth for twenty minutes, you reach a powerline. Turn left and follow the powerline on a bearing of 250° true for ten minutes to a well-defined tote road that is shown on the USGS Quadrangle east of Topknot Mountain. Turn right on it and head in a northerly direction as it winds across fairly level overgrown pasture land. Gradually the road begins to climb as you pass the slopes of Topknot Mountain on the left, west. About thirty minutes from the powerline, the tote road bends to the left to 300° true and becomes less distinct as it gradually climbs into the col between Ellenburg and Topknot mountains.

The tote road ends at an abandoned cabin in the col, about 1.5 miles from the start. From the cabin, continue northwest on a bearing of 325° true to the base of the steep part of Ellenburg. This point is about an hour and a quarter from the powerline.

Head north, 10° true, and climb the steep section through a maple forest with balsam and white birch. As you climb, bear to the right to reach an open area at 2500 feet in about twenty minutes. From here there are good views from the east through the south to the west. You can easily identify Chazy Lake, Dannemora Mountain, Topknot Mountain, Lyon Mountain, and Chateaugay Lake.

Continue more to the right on a bearing of 50° true to cross the 2597-foot minor summit. Continue through a slight col and turn left to 10° true.

After some more climbing you reach the flat top of Ellenburg Mountain at an elevation of about 2700 feet, a two hour hike from the powerline, about 2.3 miles from the road.

Ellenburg Mountain is a northeast-southwest trending ridge of granite gneiss. The steep cliffs on the southeast side of the ridge provide several opportunities for good southerly views. Be sure to allow time for a summit ridge exploration.

The return trip takes about an hour and a half. Leave the summit on a bearing of 190°. At the level area below the 2600-foot contour, turn right to 230° and continue the descent. As you descend, bear left so that you are heading south at the base of the steep section and southeast 145° as you enter the col between Ellenburg and Topknot. From the abandoned cabin, follow the tote road south to the powerline. Then follow the powerline northeast for ten minutes and bushwhack southeast to NY 374. The tote road itself ends in a private pasture behind houses on NY 374 west of the place you park to begin the bushwhack.

95 Dannemora Mountain

Bushwhack, map XXIII

Dannemora Mountain is the extension of the granite gneiss ridge that begins at Johnson Mountain to the southwest. The rocks are rich in iron ore. From the main gate in the west wall of the prison, go west on Cook Street, NY 374, following the highway as it turns north. Continue uphill and park in a parking area at a spring at 1.6 miles on the left. (There is good water at the spring.)

From the spring, walk north on NY 374 for 0.3 mile and turn right on a good tote road heading 30° true. After a couple minutes, you reach another tote road on the right. Follow it toward 110° true as it climbs steeply.

If you had continued straight on the original road, the better of the two, thirty minutes of hiking along it would bring you to a clearing used by hunters for camping. It is just to the east of the "M" in "Dannemora Mtn" on the 7.5-minute Quadrangle.

The road to the right soon turns right to 145° and reaches a height-of-land. The bushwhack begins at the height-of-land on a bearing of 60° true. Climb in this direction for fifteen minutes to an elevation of about 2200 feet. Turn right, due east, and continue across the flat eastern summit of

Dannemora Mountain. After fifteen more minutes on this bearing, you cross a small, flat valley that has a drainage flowing due south. Continue east on a bearing of 80° and cross a low hill and pass through a slight valley. The top of the next low hill is the true summit of Dannemora Mountain. In the flat center portion of the summit, you can find a 1942 survey benchmark, but there is no view from the summit. A return on a bearing of 260° takes you about forty minutes.

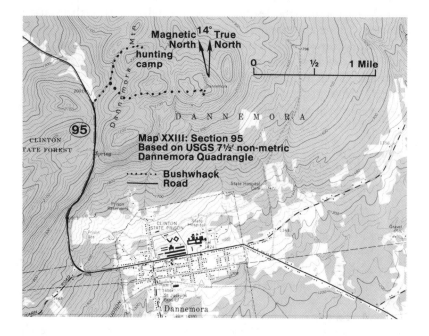

Lyon Mountain Area

Neither mine nor settlement at Lyon shows on the Beers Atlas for 1869. One of the last mines to be developed in the north country, the Chateaugay Ore Bed on Lyon Mountain was opened in 1868. The first road to Lyon Mountain was a thirteen-mile branch of the Saranac River Plank Road. Ore originally was taken to the head of Upper Chateaugay Lake, then by barge twelve miles downstream through the lakes to The Forge. In 1874, a plank road was pushed from Dannemora through twelve miles of swampy forest land to Lyon Mountain. Finally, in 1879, the Chateaugay Railroad was extended from Dannemora to Lyon Mountain. This route later went to kilns and forest land at Loon Lake, then south to Saranac Lake and Lake Placid.

In 1875, a twenty-fire Catalan forge was built on the Chateaugay River to process Lyon Mountain's ore. So rapidly did the settlement at Lyon Mountain grow that there were 700 inhabitants in 1879, 3000 by 1883. Iron was king until the 1950s. The mines closed in 1967, not because they were exhausted, but because it was cheaper to mine in Minnesota. As much as seventy-five million tons of ore remains beneath the mountain.

96 Lyon Mountain

Hiking, snowshoeing
2.2 miles, 2 hours, 1920-foot vertical rise, map XXIV

To find the Lyon Mountain Trail start at the corner of Chazy Lake Road and NY 374, 9.1 miles west of Dannemora. Go south on Chazy Lake Road and at 1.7 miles turn right, west, on a rough gravel road, which you follow for 1 mile until it ends in an informal parking area.

The trail starts at the southwest corner of the parking area at an elevation of 1900 feet. The trail is really an old tote road through an alder, striped maple, and poplar second growth forest. The tote road once served the fire tower cabin and also provided access to an old ski development that used to be located near the parking area. Although the ski trail is gradually growing back, there are places that provide good views of Lyon

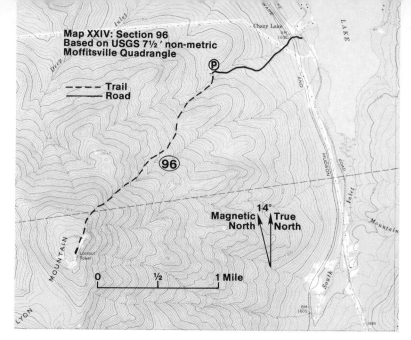

Map XXIV: Section 96
Based on USGS 7½' non-metric
Moffitsville Quadrangle

- - - - Trail
————— Road

Mountain ahead to the southwest. At 1 mile, after about forty minutes, the tote road crosses a brook flowing right to left; behind you Ellenburg Mountain is visible.

Shortly after, at an elevation of 2560 feet, the trail continues southwest while the tote road heads off to the right in a more westerly direction. In five minutes you cross a brook that flows from right to left. The trail is filled with boulders and cobbles.

The trail becomes quite steep and eroded in places. You reach the fire tower cabin site at 1.5 miles after an hour and twenty minutes. The cabin, at elevation 3130 feet, was burned by vandals in the 1970s and only the foundation remains today. The iron telephone poles remain at intervals along the route. Beyond the cabin site, the trail continues very steeply, crosses a black dike in the granite gneiss, and works its way around some huge boulders. It turns more southerly at 1.8 miles, elevation 3700 feet, about twenty minutes from the cabin site. At this point the white birch and balsam forest becomes noticeably stunted. The trail levels and some old red DEC markers appear. You reach the fire tower at 2.2 miles, about two hours from the parking area, thirty-five minutes from the cabin site.

The fire tower and the bare rocks of the summit provide excellent views of Ellenburg Mountain, Chazy Lake, and Johnson Mountain to the east. You can still see the remains of the Colvin bolt at elevation 3820 feet as well as evidence of the four iron support rings for Colvin's survey platform. At 255° the WCFE tower stands on Averill Peak.

The return to the parking area takes about an hour and a half.

97 Norton Peak and Norton Peak Caves

Bushwhack, map XXV

Norton Peak and the small caves near the top of this mountain are located on the Lyon Mountain 7.5-minute USGS.

The trip begins at the corner of NY 3 and Silver Lake Road (Clinton County Route 13) in Clayburg, which is west of Plattsburgh. Go west on NY 3 and almost immediately, at 0.1 mile, bear right on Standish Road. Follow it as it climbs through the hamlet of High Bank at 4.4 miles, and at 4.7 miles you reach an intersection with Cold Brook Road (Ruel Road) on the left and True Brook Road on the right, east. Norton Peak appears ahead to your left, northwest, and Averill Peak is ahead on the right, northeast. Continue north from High Bank, and at 6.4 miles you reach an open area on the left, west, side of Standish Road. This is immediately before Cold Brook flows under Standish Road through a large iron culvert. There is room to park several cars here.

The bushwhack begins at an elevation of about 1690 feet in an open area that was once a log landing. Head due west on a bearing of 270° true, following an overgrown roadway through alders and birch saplings. After about ten minutes, 0.25 mile, the road disappears and you enter a balsam and beech forest. Continue on the same due west bearing over a low ridge

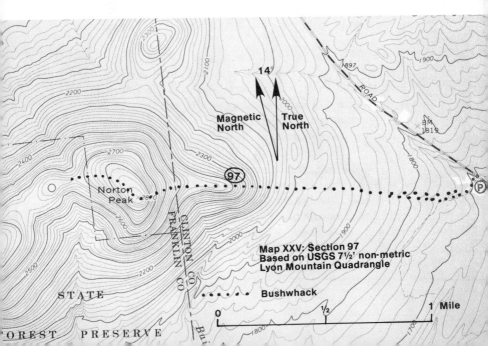

and across a north flowing drainage. Cross a second low ridge and another north flowing drainage. The route becomes steeper. Bluets and red trillium cover the forest floor among scattered boulders.

After an hour and ten minutes and nearly 1.5 miles on this due west course, you reach the 2440-foot top of a nose of high land that extends eastward from Norton Peak. The nose is a very open yellow and white birch forest. From here you can see Norton Peak through the trees. Continue on the same course due west and cross a slight col between the nose and the peak and then begin to climb again.

As you climb, bear left to reach bare open rock on the southeast corner of the peak. Ascend the bare rock to appreciate the views it provides of Averill Peak, the Champlain Valley, the Saranac River Valley, and Whiteface Mountain. From the top of the bare rock, a short bushwhack through a wind-blown white birch forest brings you to the summit. The total bushwhack covers 1.9 miles and takes an hour and forty-five minutes.

At the south end of the summit there is a small cairn with a stake held in place by guy wires. From this vantage point, the views are truly superb and unobstructed, from 30° in the northeast through the south and around to 280° in the west. The panorama includes Averill Peak, Dannemora Mountain, the Champlain Valley with Mount Mansfield and Camels Hump in the Green Mountains of Vermont beyond, the Saranac Valley, Whiteface, and the McKenzie Range. The true summit and the drill hole of a former survey mark at 2870 feet is located a short distance north of the cairn near some small white pine and spruce trees. There are no views here.

From the summit go northwest on a bearing of 300° true and descend along the west side of Norton Peak. The route goes sort of side slope down through a white birch forest. A ten-minute hike from the summit brings you to the northeast end of the broad ridge that connects the main Norton Peak with the western summit, elevation 2855 feet. Go west along this ridge, keeping 20 yards or so north of the ridge crest, and in less than ten minutes you will reach the rift that is the site of the Norton Peak caves.

The rift trends 280° and extends for about 80 yards along, and at a slight northerly angle to, the east-west ridge. The rift is irregular, averaging about twenty feet deep and twenty feet across. At both the east and west ends there is a place on the north side of the rift where it is possible to descend into it. The west entrance was iced during a spring visit and would have required crampons and a safety belay rope. The east entrance

Ice in entrance to cave on Norton Peak

descends north along a joint plane in the rock over a short pitch, then turns west, left, to bring you to a small room about twenty feet high, five feet across, and twenty yards long. Vandals have spray-painted graffiti on the wall. To the west, the room ends.

The rift appears to represent the colluvial movement of a large block of Lyon Mountain granite gneiss along three main sets of joint planes in the rock. The cause of movement is probably due to the near-horizontal joint planes that dip down slope to the north. Water percolating into the near-horizontal joint planes acts as a lubricant to allow a large block to slide downhill to the north. As it slides on the horizontal joint planes, the caves are opened up, primarily along the east-west trending vertical joint planes and to a lesser extent along the north-south trending vertical joint planes.

After exploring the caves, retrace your route back to Standish Road. First head due east along the ridge. You may see some faded blue paint blazes and some old red painted tin can lids. Ignore these. As you begin to climb Norton Peak, shift your bearing to the southeast at 120°. After hiking fifteen minutes from the caves, you reach the summit of Norton Peak. Continue across the peak to the cairn at the south end. From here head off the summit on a bearing of due east. You will cross the nose on the east side about twenty minutes after leaving the summit. Continue off the nose on a bearing of 90° and cross the same drainages you crossed on the way in. With luck you may pick up the tote road for the last ten minutes. In any case, you should reach Standish Road after about an hour and a quarter descent from the summit.

The Gulf

THE GULF IS a fascinating chasm that trends generally east-west along the United States-Canada border in northern Clinton County, outside the Adirondack Park. It was eroded by glacial meltwater that drained Lake Iroquois, the glacial lake that occupied the Lake Ontario basin. Lake Iroquois drained into Lake Vermont that occupied what is now the whole Lake Champlain Basin during the Covey Hill stage of glacial meltback about 12,200 years ago. Because the ice dammed the lake to the north, Lake Vermont drained south down the Hudson Valley.

As the glacial meltwater from Lake Iroquois flowed into Lake Vermont, it swept the bedrock of the region around Cannon's Corners clear of soil and perhaps, catastrophically, cut the rock-walled gorge called The Gulf. As the ice continued to melt back, the water passage through the Gulf was later abandoned.

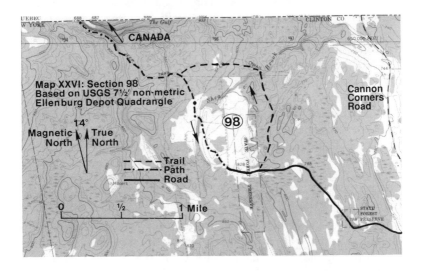

98   Gulf Unique Area Trail

Hiking, geological expedition
5.2-mile loop, 3 hours, relatively level, map XXVI

The trip to The Gulf begins at Cannon Corners at the intersection of Davison and Cannon Corners Road in the northwest corner of the Altona 7.5-minute Quadrangle. Go north on Cannon Corner Road and turn left 1.1 miles from Davison Road onto Rock Road, which is a good gravel road running directly on bedrock some of the time. Rock Road soon crosses into the Ellenburgh Depot 7.5-minute Quadrangle.

Rock Road continues west and northwest. You reach a small parking area on the right at 2.6 miles. This spot is the trailhead for the Unique Area; you can drive another 0.3 mile to a locked gate, but there is no parking at the gate, so you must park at the trailhead.

Red DEC markers lead you from the parking area northeast along the trail. The trail crosses the red sandstones of the Potsdam Group which were laid down in a late Cambrian marine environment over 500 million years ago. You drop over small sandstone ledges in a white pine forest. After a few minutes, the trail bends left and takes a more northerly direction. You pass a wetland on the left and cross its outlet on a wood bridge about 0.6 mile from the parking area. The trail continues generally northwest and crosses two drainages on wood bridges before crossing Shea Brook on a bridge, at 1.0 mile, about thirty minutes from the parking area.

Shortly beyond Shea Brook, the trail turns left and heads due west through alders. It bends left, along an old jeep trail for a short distance, then leaves the jeep trail going on a bearing of true west. After crossing other jeep trails and log roads, the hiking trail ends at a gravel road, at 1.7 miles, about one hour from the parking area.

Turn right onto the gravel road and follow it as it climbs slightly in a general westerly direction. Stay on the road and pass a section of fence on the right. The land is posted for a short distance by the Gulf View Club, but public access along the roadway is permitted under an easement agreement; the trail returns to state land in 0.2 mile.

The road generally bends more northwesterly as it twists and turns northwesterly and eventually reaches open bedrock. At 2.5 miles, about an hour and a half from the parking lot, the steep chasm that is The Gulf begins to appear to the right (north) of the road. The trail continues northwest along the southwest edge of The Gulf. In another fifteen minutes at 2.8 miles, you reach the United States-Canada border Monument No. 688, one of the chain of monuments that mark the border. The border is a cleared swath through the forest and you can see The Gulf to the east of the monument. Walk to the edge of The Gulf; you can see Monument No. 687 on the other side, and you have a remarkable view of the sheer sandstone walls of the chasm. There is a herd path along the edge of The Gulf that can be followed to the southeast for about 0.2 mile; it offers a variety of perspectives of The Gulf and the floating bog in the deep lake that occupies it.

To return to the parking area, follow the gravel road for 1.1 miles, thirty minutes back to the red DEC trail that comes in on the left. To make a loop trip on the road, continue south and southeast past the DEC trail. After ten minutes the road bends sharply left and crosses Shea Brook on a dam that creates a small farm pond. The road continues southeast past a cultivated field and fifteen minutes beyond Shea Brook you reach a locked gate. Beyond are some farm buildings at the end of town-maintained Rock Road, and in five minutes you are at the parking area. The return from the intersection this way is 1.2 miles, 0.4 mile shorter than the marked trail.

The Gulf is three-quarters of a mile wide, over two miles long, with a maximum depth of over a thousand feet. It is theorized that the upper portion of its V-shaped walls were cut by glacial scouring while the lower portion was cut by meltwaters that flowed through the valley as the glacier retreated. Today the floor of the Gulf is nearly flat and filled with elongated beaver ponds and swamps surrounding a small stream that contrasts vividly with the surging river that needed to created The Gulf.

References and Other Resources

References

DeSormo, Maitland C. *The Heydays of the Adirondacks*. Saranac Lake, New York: Adirondack Yesteryears, Inc. 1974.

Donaldson, Alfred L. *A History of the Adirondacks*, Volumes I and II. Harrison, New York: Harbor Hill Books, 1977 reprint of 1921 edition, published by Century and Co., New York.

Franklin Historical Review, Franklin County Historical and Museum Society, Volume 1, 1964 to Volume 24, 1987.

Gallos, Phil. *By Foot in the Adirondacks*. Guidebook compiled from newspaper column in the *Adirondack Daily Enterprise*, Saranac Lake, New York: Adirondack Publishing Company, 1972.

Gallos, Phil. *Cure Cottages of Saranac Lake – Architecture and History of a Pioneer Health Resort*. Historic Saranac, 1985.

Hardy, Philip. *The Iron Age Community of the J&J Rogers Iron Company in the Ausable Valley, New York, 1825-1900*. Ph.D. Dissertation, Bowling Green University, 1985. University Microfilms, Ann Arbor, Michigan.

Hough, Franklin B., M. D. *A History of St. Lawrence and Franklin Counties, New York*. Originally published Albany, 1853. Facsimile Edition, St. Lawrence Historical Society and Franklin County Historical and Museum Society, Baltimore: Regional Publishing Co. 1970.

Hurd, Duane H. *History of Clinton and Franklin Counties, New York*. Originally published Philadelphia, Pennsylvania, 1880. Facsimile Edition, Clinton County American Revolution Bicentennial Commission, Plattsburgh, New York, 1978.

Jamieson, Paul. *Adirondack Canoe Waters, North Flow*. Glens Falls, New York: Adirondack Mountain Club, 1975, revised 1981.

Kudish, Michael. *Where Did the Tracks Go*. Saranac Lake, New York: The Chauncey Press, 1985.

Miller, William J. *Geology of the Lyon Mountain Quadrangle*. New York State Museum and Science Service Bulletin 271, 1926.

Moravek, John Richard. *The Iron Industry as a geographic force in the Adirondacks and Champlain Region of New York State, 1800-1971*. Ph.D.

Dissertation, University of Tennessee, 1976. University Microfilms, Ann Arbor, Michigan.

North Country Notes, Clinton County Historical Association, Issue No. 1, November 1960 through Issue No. 238, December 1987.

Tyler, Helen Escha. *Mountain Memories, Folk Tales of the Adirondacks.* Saranac Lake, New York: The Currier Press, 1974.

Other Resources

Cross-Country Ski Trails, Town of Harrietstown, available at Dewey Mountain Saranac Lake, New York.

The Jackrabbit Trail, Linking Keene, Lake Placid, Saranac Lake, and the High Peaks Region, Adirondack Ski Touring Council, P.O. Box 843, Lake Placid, New York, 12946.

New York State Department of Environmental Conservation, Region 5, Ray Brook, 518-835-1370.

DEC Booklets:
 Nordic Skiing Trails in New York State
 Snowmobiling in New York State

Pitchoff bluffs

Index

Guidebooks from Countryman Press and Backcountry Publications

Written for people of all ages and experience, these popular and carefully prepared books feature detailed trail and tour directions, notes on points of interest and natural highlights, maps, and photographs.

Discover the Adirondacks Series
Discover the Adirondack High Peaks, $14.95
Discover the Central Adirondacks, Second Edition $12.95
Discover the Eastern Adirondacks, $10.95
Discover the Northeastern Adirondacks, $1.95
Discover the Northern Adirondacks, $12.95
Discover the Northwestern Adirondacks, $12.95
Discover the South Central Adirondacks, $10.95
Discover the Southeastern Adirondacks, $9.95
Discover the Southern Adirondacks, $10.95
Discover the Southwestern Adirondacks, $9.95
Discover the West Central Adirondacks, $14.95

Other Guides to New York State
Canoeing Central New York, $10.95
Fifty Hikes in the Adirondacks, Second Edition $12.95
Fifty Hikes in Central New York, $11.95
Fifty Hikes in the Hudson Valley, $12.95
Fifty Hikes in Western New York, $12.95
20 Bicycle Tours in the Finger Lakes, Second Edition $9.95
20 Bicycle Tours in the Five Boroughs (NYC), $8.95
20 Bicycle Tours in and around New York City, $9.00
25 Bicycle Tours in the Hudson Valley, $9.95
Walks & Rambles in Dutchess and Putnam Counties (NY), $10.95

Our outdoor recreation guides are available through bookstores and specialty shops. For a free catalog on these and other books, please write: The Countryman Press, Inc., Dept. APC, PO Box 175, Woodstock, VT 05091.

Patricia Collier, has four great loves: mountains, music, people, and books—not necessarily in that order. She is a peace and social justice activist and has spent years fighting for this planet's environment and, more specifically, for the protection of her beloved Adirondacks. She is an Adirondack 46er and has been active in the Adirondack Mountain Club for 18 years. She has only 16 mountains remaining in order to complete the 111 high peaks in the northeast—10 in New Hampshire and 6 in Maine. Pat has seven grown children and has spent most of her life in New York State.

Photo by Caroline Dawson

Peter O'Shea is a retired police sergeant who has become very involved in environmental issues in the north country. He serves on the board of directors of the local Audubon Society and the Indian Creek Nature Center. He has written for *Adirondac* magazine and other Adirondack Mountain Club publications. Peter is an avid and knowledgeable student of Adirondack wildlife and is an active member of the New York Chapter of the Wildlife Society. He serves on a subcommittee advising the state on land acquisition.

James C. Dawson and his wife, Caroline, are outdoor enthusiasts who enjoy hiking, canoeing, cross-country skiing, and fishing in the Adirondacks, as well as sailing on Lake Champlain. Jim is a professor at the Center for Earth and Environmental Science, State University of New York at Plattsburgh, and his expertise as a geologist has enriched this series. Jim is well known as an active conservationist. He chairs the Adirondack Land Trust, is President of the Association for the Protection of the Adirondacks, is New York Chair of the Lake Champlain Committee, and is active in several other organizations dedicated to preserving New York's wilderness environment.

Photo by Pat Collier